Cheat's Cuisine

For François and Míla with a bellyful of love

First published in 2007 by
CURRACH PRESS
55A Spruce Avenue, Stillorgan Industrial Park,
Blackrock, Co. Dublin

www.currach.ie
1 3 5 4 2

Photography by Christian O'Brien
Cover photographs by Christian O'Brien
Design and layout by Richard Parfrey
Cover design by Richard Parfrey
Printed by Estudios Gráficos Zure, Bilbao, Spain

ISBN: 978-1-85607-951-8

JUL 2008

Cheat's Cuisine

Dinner for 6 in 60 minutes

CURRACH PRESS

Introduction

It was Frank Coughlan from the *Irish Independent* who approached me about writing a column for the paper's Saturday magazine. He had this quirky idea for me to devise a dinner menu for six people that could be cooked in sixty minutes – Cheat's Cusine. Of course I jumped at the challenge and, two years and over three hundred recipes later, the Saturday column is still going strong. This book is a collection of some of the best published Cheat's Cusine recipes and some new recipes that will, I hope, make cooking for family, friends or even a sophisticated dinner party seem a lot easier.

Each menu is themed to make it easy for you to choose what type of dinner you want to create. I have also given a price guide to help with your decision. With each menu I have given timing instructions so that the recipes can be easily followed. The names of the dishes and the lists of ingredients are colour-matched to the instructions for each part of the menu.

Since starting the column I have had great fun creating, testing and tasting the dishes. I get most of my ideas from friends and family (some of you are mentioned in the short introduction to each menu) and as always I am truly grateful. We have had some fun dinner parties over the years and I thank all those who came to test the menus.

In creating *Cheat's Cuisine* I had great help from many people. I wish to thank the team involved in producing this book: my editor Fiona Biggs, Richard Parfrey for the design, Chris O'Brien for his enthusiasm and patience in taking all the photos, Teresa Daly for the hard job ahead of press and publicity, and Jo O'Donoghue, publisher at Currach Press, for taking on the project and being so understanding during any difficulties.

This also gives me the opportunity to show my appreciation for the wonderful support I have always received from the team at Saturday's *Irish Independent*. Thanks to Frank Coughlan, executive editor of features and magazines, for giving me a wonderful gig; to Bairbre Power, editor of the *Weekend Magazine*; and to Helen Hanley, Paul Whittington, Gabriel Bruton, Sophie Gorman, all of whom had the job of editing my column and some of whom have moved on to other things. *Go raibh míle maith agaibh*!

A special thank you to Annie (Andgana Matramuc), who not only took great care of Míla, giving me time to write and create recipes, but was a great kitchen buddy, helping me to test and taste all the recipes. This leads me on to farm manager Paddy Kelly, whose taste buds were very influential in selecting recipes for this book. If his reply was 'pure lush' it's in the book.

Merci beaucoup to Tiffany from Blue Door, Naas, for lending me some of the items used in the photographs and for her stylish input.

A big thank you also to my friends and family: Mum, Papa, Grandma G, Caoimhín, Siobhan, Ghislain and Françoise Drion and all the Drion family. Simon Wells, Sue Keating, Kathleen and Remi Dillon, Kari Rocca and Barry McCall, Tara and Mark Butterly, Kate McColgan and Anne Kennedy, Colette and Simon Cully, Arthur Craigie, Catherine Walsh, John de Robeck for his pork, Nolans of Kilcullen for supplying the best meat in the country, Neil McGrath for all the game and fish – I love coming home to find dead ducks in my sink! Jenny and Richard from the Grangecon Café for all the great ideas, Siobhán Popewell for running the farmers' market, Mary Kingston and Brian Graham, Sheila Rasmussen and Johnny Williams. Thanks to all of you for making me laugh and cry, and being the best testers and tasters.

By the way, a big thanks to my dear François for leaving me something to eat, doing the washing up and taking such great care of our daughter.

Dia libh

Buon Appetito

And *sláinte mhaith* to Frank Coughlan, who started it all.

Aoileann Garavaglia
Co Kildare
October 2007

Please note

All the recipes contained in this book serve six people.

The euro sign at the start of each menu indicates how much it is likely to cost: € = economical; €€= moderately expensive; €€€ = expensive; €€€€ = extravagant.

The names of the dishes and the lists of ingredients are colour-matched to the instructions for each part of the menu.

A teaspoon is 5ml; a tablespoon is 15ml.

Eggs and individual vegetables and pieces of fruit are medium, unless otherwise stated.

Salt is assumed to be coarse sea salt and pepper is assumed to be freshly ground black pepper, unless otherwise stated.

Raw and lightly cooked eggs should be avoided by infants, the elderly, pregnant women, anyone suffering from an illness or convalescing, and anyone with a weakened immune system.

People with nut allergies should be aware that some of the readymade products recommended in this book may contain nuts.

Winter

Kitchen Table Supper 12

Roast chicken with rosemary and lemon,
celeriac gratin and roast tomatoes

Cheese and a crisp green salad

Chocolate mousse with whiskey cream

One-Pot Winter Warmer 17

Carrot and beetroot crisps with
a spicy pepper and tomato dip

Smoked fish and fennel stew

Lemon mascarpone sweet tartlets

Grandma Garavaglia's Meatballs 19

Rocket and Parma ham salad
with a honey and lemon dressing

Meatballs with spaghetti and garlic bread

Vanilla ice cream

Alternative Christmas Dinner! 23

Aperitif with a selection of olives

Venison sausages with red onion marmalade
and a gratin of sweet potatoes

Cranberry fruit salad with meringue nests

Cook to Impress! 26

Baked plaice with a chilli
vinaigrette and rustic bread

Linguine with mussels in tomato sauce

**Pears poached in red wine on
meringue with crème fraîche**

North African Twist 30

Mozzarella salad with a walnut dressing

Grilled fillet steak with cumin- and
coriander-roasted carrot and potato

Ginger cake

Sunday Curry 33

Aperitif with Bombay mix

Spicy lamb curry with dates,
almonds and couscous

Lemon and mango sorbet

New Year's Eve Dinner 36

Aperitif with oysters

Roast duck breast with a honey and ginger
sauce, roast sweet potatoes and spinach

Lemon mousse with Champagne raspberries

Family Lunch 41

Mushroom soup

Baked salmon with Joan's sauce,
served with baby potatoes and peas

**Vanilla ice cream with a berry coulis
and a vanilla shortbread biscuit**

Game Season Feast 45

Bresaola with rocket

Pheasant casseroled in cider
with roast potato wedges

Poached pears in honey and cardamom

The Best Fish Dish 47

Lemon and herb salad with creamy
goat's cheese croûtons

Baked whole sea bass
with fennel and tomatoes

Amaretti crunch ice cream with a mango coulis

Winter in the Med 51

Baked goat's cheese in a walnut crust
on a bed of herb salad with walnut dressing

Striploin steak with ratatouille

Baked apples with sweet walnuts

Spring

Oriental Flair — 56
Orange ginger chicken
with cashew nuts and rice
Warm peach pudding with vanilla cream

Cooking with Kids — 61
Italian antipasti
Ricotta and spinach cannelloni
Crisp garden salad
Vanilla ice cream with a sweet raspberry sauce

Indian Feast — 64
Chicken korma with homemade naan
breads, served with chutney and a
cucumber and red onion salsa
Fresh pineapple

Asian Fusion — 69
Asian-style fish cakes with dipping sauce
Stir-fried pork with mixed
vegetables and oyster sauce
Fresh fruit

Mexican Fiesta with Margaritas — 73
Tortilla chips with homemade salsa
Steak fajitas with guacamole,
soured cream and salsa
**Aunt Linda's golden Californian
classic margaritas**

Family Sunday Lunch — 76
Warm tomato tartlets
Plaice with herb butter
and almond green beans
Vanilla ice cream with apricot sauce

Everyday Light Supper — 81
Smoked pancetta and leek quiche
Garden herb salad
Lemon and raspberry cream pots

Comfort Night In — 84
Chicory wrapped in ham
and baked in white sauce
Crisp green salad
Apple tartlets with vanilla ice cream

His and Hers Movie Night In — 87
Avocado salad
Spaghetti alla carbonara
Apple and plum pecan crumble with cream

Midweek recovery meal — 91
Black pudding salad
with tomato relish and soldiers
Lamb stew
Irish whiskey bread and butter pudding

Mother's Day Lunch — 93
Pea and mint soup with a vanilla froth
Herb-crusted cod with boiled
potatoes and Joan's sauce
Lemon curd sponge cake

Garden Party — 97
Françoise's mackerel pâté on rye toast
Fresh herb pasta
**Homemade meringue with
strawberries and cream**

Summer

Autumn

Warm Weekend Evening   140
Figs with Parma ham

Grilled mackerel fillets with a
lemon caper butter dressing

Pineapple caramelised in white rum

Family Reunion   143
Raclette with salad

Blackberry and almond tortaline

Sunday Game   146
Aperitif with a selection of olives

Tagliatelle with blue cheese and a crisp green
salad with a raspberry vinaigrette dressing

Sweet almond and orange cake

Making an Impression   149
Aperitif with a mixture of nuts
and small crackers

Asian salmon parcels with a
soy and ginger sauce

Autumn fruits trifle

Lunch for the Girls   152
Aperitif with cashew nuts

Annie's aubergine, courgette and
goat's cheese filo loaf and a green salad
with a sweet balsamic dressing

Sticky toffee muffins with toffee
sauce and vanilla ice cream

Lunch for Mother-in-Law   156
Aperitif with a selection of olives

Lemon paprika chicken
with long-grain and wild rice

Mixed leaf salad

Apple and ricotta pastry parcels

Bloke's Night In   160
Chicken wings

Texas chilli served with tortillas

Casual Midweek Dinner   163
Lamb chops with roast vegetables,
new potatoes and Dijon mustard

Cashel Blue, blueberry and walnut salad

Meringue nests with ricotta vanilla cream
and fresh fruit with a blueberry coulis

Candlelight Dinner   167
Aperitif with prawn crackers and
a sweet chilli dipping sauce

Sweet chilli salmon cakes, coriander rice with
a teriyaki chilli sauce and baby spinach

Vanilla and apricot compôte
with vanilla ice cream

Alternative Sunday Dinner   171
Meatloaf with roast potatoes, broccoli
and a comforting white sauce

Apple pie

Something a Bit Cheffy   175
Chicken breast stuffed with Brie and
leeks, wrapped in smoked pancetta

Green salad with a French dressing

Lemon syllabub

Oozing Sophistication   179
Poulet au vin

Salad with cheese

Quitterie's chocolate fondants
and vanilla ice cream

Winter

Kitchen Table Supper

€   The main course is light enough and the social aspect of picking at cheese with salad is a nice way to enjoy good company. The mousse may seem a little tricky at first but I guarantee that once you've made it for the first time, this dessert will be a staple for any occasion. The cheese and salad before dessert is the French way. Try it and enjoy!

Roast chicken with rosemary and lemon, celeriac gratin and roast tomatoes

Cheese and a crisp green salad

Chocolate mousse with whiskey cream

6 portions chicken leg
    with thigh attached

3 tbsp olive oil

handful fresh rosemary sprigs

2 lemons

Celeriac gratin

1 celeriac

1 tbsp olive oil

2 garlic cloves, crushed

100g Parmesan cheese, grated

150ml single cream

salt and pepper

Roast tomatoes

6 tomatoes

olive oil, for drizzling

1 tbsp fennel seeds

1 tsp runny honey

salt and pepper

selection of cheeses (Cashel
    Blue, Carrigbyrne, St
    Killians, Gubbeen)

water biscuits

2 heads lettuce (different types)

Dressing

6 tbsp olive oil

2 tbsp red wine vinegar

1 tsp runny honey

1 tsp Dijon mustard

salt and pepper

175g good quality
    plain chocolate

200ml double cream

4 eggs

50g icing sugar

150ml single cream

1 tbsp whiskey

1 tsp soft light brown sugar

instant coffee granules
    or grated chocolate,
    for decorating

0–10 minutes	*For the chicken:* Preheat the oven to 200°C/400°F/Gas Mark 6. Place the chicken portions in a single layer on a baking dish. Drizzle with olive oil. Scatter the sprigs of fresh rosemary on top. Cut the lemons into quarters. Squeeze 2 quarters over the chicken portions, then scatter the remaining quarters among them. Season with salt and pepper and place in the oven for about 55–60 minutes.
	Melt the chocolate in a heatproof bowl placed over a saucepan of boiling water. Whisk the double cream until it forms soft peaks.
10–20 minutes	Separate the eggs. Whisk the egg whites to stiff peaks, then add the icing sugar and whisk until the sugar is mixed in. Using a fork, beat the egg yolks, then add the cooled melted chocolate to the beaten yolks and gently stir.
20–30 minutes	Using a large metal spoon, fold 1 tablespoon of the whipped cream into the chocolate to loosen it. Fold in the remaining cream. Using a metal spoon, fold in 1 tablespoon of the egg white into the chocolate mixture. Add the remaining egg white carefully, folding so that you keep air in the mousse. Divide the mixture between 6 small wine glasses and leave to chill in the fridge.
30–40 minutes	*For the gratin:* Place the bottom part of a steamer on the hob to heat. Trim the outer edge of the celeriac. Using a sharp knife or food processor, thinly slice the celeriac,

place in the steamer and steam for about 5 minutes. Drizzle the oil over the base of an ovenproof baking dish. Spread out half the steamed celeriac over the base of the dish. Sprinkle over the garlic and half the Parmesan cheese and season with salt and pepper. Spread the remaining celeriac on top. Pour over the cream. Sprinkle the top with the remaining Parmesan cheese. Cover with foil and set aside.

For the tomatoes: Cut each tomato in half around the equator, halfway between the stem end and the base. Arrange the tomatoes, cut side up, in a small ovenproof dish. Drizzle with olive oil and scatter fennel seeds evenly over the tomatoes. Season with salt and pepper and drizzle with honey.

40–50 minutes

Put the gratin and the tomatoes in the oven.

Mix all the ingredients for the dressing together in a jar. Arrange the cheese on a plate and leave to stand at room temperature.

50–60 minutes

Remove the foil from the celeriac and allow to brown for the last 10 minutes of cooking. Remove the chicken from the oven. By now it should have been cooking for at least 55 minutes. Remove the tomatoes from the oven.

Serve each person a portion of chicken and two tomato halves. Put the gratin on the table and allow your guests to serve themselves.

To serve

When the main course is finished, put the cheese plate on the table and toss the salad leaves with the some of the dressing. The amount of dressing you use depends upon the quantity of salad.

About 5 minutes before you serve the dessert whip the cream until it forms soft peaks, then add the whiskey and the sugar. Remove the chocolate mousse from the fridge and place a large dollop of whiskey cream on top. Decorate with a pinch of coffee granules and serve immediately.

Unoaked Chardonnay
Côtes du Rhône

...and to drink

One-Pot Winter Warmer

This stew is ideal for dinner or even lunch on a cold winter's day. My 16-month-old niece, Améli, loved it, all mashed up.

€€–€€€

Carrot and beetroot crisps
with a spicy pepper and tomato dip

Smoked fish and fennel stew

Lemon mascarpone sweet tartlets

1 packet carrot crisps

1 packet beetroot crisps

bottled stir-through spicy
   pepper and tomato sauce

2 onions

3–4 carrots

2 garlic cloves

2 fennel bulbs

1kg baby potatoes (Agata)

800g canned organic tomatoes

1 tbsp organic tomato purée

2 tbsp olive oil

1 tsp mixed herbs

2 bay leaves

1 litre vegetable stock or
   1 organic vegetable
   stock cube, made up to
   1 litre with hot water

1kg mussels

large piece chunky
   cod, about 300g

2 large salmon fillets,
   about 400g in total

smoked haddock, about
   400g in total

salt and pepper

75g Parmesan cheese,
   grated, and 230ml double
   cream, to serve

handful flaked almonds

**320–460g good quality
   lemon curd**

250g mascarpone cheese

6 pre-baked tartlet cases

blueberries, to decorate

Roughly chop the onions. Cut the carrots into chunky rounds. Chop the garlic. Cut the tops off the fennel bulbs and roughly slice the bulbs. Cut the potatoes in half.

0–10 minutes

Heat the oil in a large casserole dish, add the onion and garlic and sweat for about 4 minutes. Add the carrots and fennel, tossing them with the onion and garlic.

10–20 minutes

20–30 minutes	Add the canned tomatoes and tomato purée and mix well. Season with salt and pepper and add the mixed herbs and the bay leaves. Finally, add the potatoes, then the stock, cover the dish and cook over a medium heat for about 20 minutes.
30–40 minutes	Preheat the oven to 190°C/375°F/Gas Mark 5. Wash the mussels under cold running water, then scrub them and remove the beards. Skin the fish and cut into large chunks.
40–50 minutes	Place the almonds on a baking tray and toast in the oven until they begin to brown.
	In a clean bowl mix the mascarpone cheese with 320–400g of the lemon curd. Taste and add more lemon curd, if you like. I love these tartlets really lemony so I tend to use 430–460g lemon curd. Spoon the cheese mixture into the tartlet cases. Using the back of a teaspoon swirl the cheese in a circular motion to make it look decorative. Sprinkle a few flaked almonds on top of each tartlet and decorate with a blueberry. Set aside the tartlets in a cool place.
50–60 minutes	Give the soup a stir. Add the fish and cook over a low heat for about 5 minutes, then add the mussels and replace the lid. Cook over a medium heat for a further 2 minutes. Remove from the heat but leave the lid on until you are ready to serve. The mussels should all have opened up by now. Discard any that remain closed.
To serve	Serve the crisps with the sauce as a dip.
	Place a bowl of grated Parmesan cheese and a jug of pouring cream on the table. Serve each person a bowl of soup and allow each person to add his or her own cheese and cream. If they like spicy food you can put a bottle of Tabasco sauce on the table.
	Serve each person a tartlet.
...and to drink	*Chablis Premier Cru, Chardonnay or, if you prefer red, a Barbera*

Grandma Garavaglia's Meatballs

This is a real comfort meal. Every summer when we visited my grandmother in California this was the meal she would prepare for our arrival. Knowing that I was going to have spaghetti and meatballs when we got to California made the long plane journey that bit more bearable. My friends hound me for this recipe, so here it is.

Rocket and Parma ham salad with a honey and lemon dressing

Meatballs with spaghetti and garlic bread

Vanilla ice cream

1 large tbsp runny honey

100g rocket

100g red seedless
    grapes, halved

18 slices of Parma ham
    (allow 3 per person)

handful pine kernels,
    for sprinkling

juice of 1 lemon

olive oil

pepper

2 slices white bread,
    crusts removed

100ml milk

2 onions, finely chopped

olive oil

1 garlic clove, crushed

300g lean minced beef

300g lean minced pork
    (sausage meat will do)

2 tsp caraway seeds

1 egg, beaten (optional)

semolina, to coat

600g dried spaghetti

salt and pepper

freshly grated Parmesan,
    to serve

Sauce

400g canned chopped
    organic tomatoes

680g passata

2 garlic cloves, crushed

1 tsp caster sugar

2 tsp dried oregano

salt and pepper

Garlic bread

50g butter, softened

4 garlic cloves, crushed

handful chopped parsley

1 baguette

pepper

Tear the bread into chunks, place in a bowl with the milk and set aside to soften for about 3 minutes. Heat a little oil in a frying pan, add the onions and soften. Set aside to

0–10 minutes

cool before you add them to the meat.

10–20 minutes   Add the meat, onions, garlic and caraway seeds to the softened bread. Mix, kneading the mixture with your hands, so that the bread is absorbed by the other ingredients. Season to taste with salt and pepper. If necessary, add just enough egg to bind the mixture without it becoming too sloppy.

20–30 minutes   *For the sauce*: Combine the tomatoes, passata, crushed garlic, sugar and oregano in a large saucepan. Simmer over a low heat for about 10–15 minutes. To form the meatballs, fill a bowl with cold water and cover a plate with semolina. Dip your hands in the cold water (this will prevent the meat mixture becoming too messy) and then roll into walnut-sized balls. Roll each ball in the semolina to coat.

30–40 minutes   Place a large frying pan over a medium heat. Add the oil. When it is hot, add the meatballs in a single layer. They should sizzle immediately. Resist moving them around, but allow them to brown on the underside before you start to move them. It should take about 2–3 minutes to brown one side, then move them around to brown all over. Place the browned meatballs in the tomato sauce and simmer for 20 minutes.

40–50 minutes   *For the garlic bread*: Preheat the oven to 180°C/350°F/Gas Mark 4. Mix the butter with the garlic and parsley. Season with pepper. Cut slices into the top along the length of the French stick about every 3cm and then cut through each slice to a depth of two thirds of the loaf. Spread the garlic butter on both sides of each slice. Wrap the whole loaf in foil and place in the oven for 10–15 minutes.

50–60 minutes   Slightly heat the honey in a saucepan. Put the rocket and grapes into a large bowl. Pour over the honey and toss gently with your fingers. Spread out the ingredients on a large serving plate and arrange the Parma ham on top. Drizzle with lemon juice and a little olive oil and season with lots of pepper. Sprinkle with the pine kernels.

Put a large saucepan of lightly salted water on to boil.

To serve   Place the salad in the centre of the table and allow your guests to serve themselves.

About 10 minutes before you are ready to eat, add the spaghetti to the saucepan of boiling water. Boil until *al dente*, then drain and return to the saucepan. Tip the meatballs and sauce over the pasta, toss and serve.

Place some grated Parmesan cheese on the table for everyone to help themselves.

Serve each person a portion of ice cream.

...and to drink   *Prosecco, to start*
Medium-bodied red,
such as Cabernet,
Rubesco, Barbera or
Zinfandel

Alternative Christmas Dinner!

It was Sue Keating, a good friend of my mother's, who introduced me to a winter fruit salad. I have created my own version, which includes other berries, but the basic ingredient – cranberries – still remains the same. I now stock up on cranberries around Christmas and freeze them so I can make this delicious salad all year round. The gratin of sweet potato was originally made for my 12-month-old daughter Míla. Alas, she was not that fond of it, but François and I ate the lot and thought it went very well with the venison sausages.

€€

Aperitif with a selection of olives

Venison sausages with red onion marmalade and a gratin of sweet potatoes

---

Cranberry fruit salad with meringue nests

Selection of olives	Gratin of sweet potatoes	400ml water
	1kg sweet potatoes	150g sugar
5 red onions	3 tbsp olive oil, plus	340g cranberries
25g butter	extra for greasing	125g blueberries
1 sprig thyme	3 garlic cloves, finely chopped	200g red seedless
1 tbsp brown sugar	1 tsp cinnamon	grapes, halved
300ml red wine	250ml single cream	6 pre-baked meringue nests
50ml red wine vinegar	salt and pepper	organic half-fat crème
12 venison sausages		fraîche, to serve
salt and pepper		

For the gratin: Peel the sweet potatoes and, using a food processor, thinly slice them. Preheat the oven to 180°C/350°F/Gas Mark 5.

0–10 minutes

In a large mixing bowl toss the sweet potato slices in the oil, garlic, cinnamon and cream. Lightly grease a large gratin dish. Spread out the sweet potato slices in the dish. Season to taste with salt and pepper. Pour over any of the remaining cream from the bowl. Place in the oven and bake for about 40 minutes, until the sweet potato is tender and the top is browned and crisp.

10–20 minutes

For the red onion marmalade: Finely slice the onion. Heat the butter in a saucepan and add the onions and thyme. Cook over a medium heat for about 10 minutes until the onions are soft and just starting to brown.

20–30 minutes

Add the sugar, red wine and vinegar, bring to just under the boil and reduce the heat. Season with a little pepper and simmer for 30 minutes, until all the liquid has evaporated.

30–40 minutes

Place the sausages on a baking tray in the oven.

40–50 minutes

Make a sugar syrup by heating the water with the sugar in a large saucepan. When the sugar has dissolved add the cranberries and allow them to pop.

Check the potatoes. Using a spatula, turn the sausages.

50–60 minutes

When most of the cranberries have popped, remove from the heat and leave to cool for about 5 minutes. Add the rest of the berries and the grapes and stir. Set aside.

Remove the onion marmalade from the hob.

Serve the olives with some drinks.

To serve

Serve each person 2 sausages with some onion marmalade and place the gratin of sweet potato on the table.

Fill each meringue nest with some of the cooled berry mixture, top with a dollop of crème fraîche and serve immediately.

Big red, such as Bordeaux or red Zinfandel

...and to drink

Cook to Impress!

€€

Even when we were very young my brother Caoimhín had a certain flair for cooking. He was very adventurous and would love to cook things like quails'eggs, frogs' legs and snails. You name it, he cooked it. Mussels were a particular speciality of his. I have adapted one of his regular meals to suit all. The mussels not only taste great – with their juicy yellow orange flesh they look fantastic when cooked. Served simply with some pasta they make an impressive meal. Do make sure to get your mussels from a reputable fishmonger as the last thing you want is mussels that don't open. The poached pears are an elegant, sophisticated dessert, a delight after any meal. I served these one New Year's Eve.

Baked plaice with a chilli vinaigrette and rustic bread

Linguine with mussels in tomato sauce

Pears poached in red wine on meringue with crème fraîche

800g plaice fillets, about
   3 large fillets
chopped red chillies, to garnish
1 stick rustic French
   bread, to serve

Chilli vinaigrette
4–5 tbsp olive oil
juice of 1 lemon
2 scallions (spring
   onions), chopped
1 small red chilli

3 tbsp olive oil
2 onions, finely chopped
3 garlic cloves, finely chopped
800g canned chopped
   organic tomatoes
140g tomato purée
1 tsp sugar
1 tsp Italian seasoning
handful fresh basil
2kg mussels (farmed are fine)
700g dried linguine
salt
chopped fresh parsley,
   to garnish

1kg Conference pears,
   about 8 pears
400ml red wine
1 tsp cinnamon
6 cloves
2 tbsp runny honey
juice and whole peel
   of 1 clementine
6 pre-baked meringue nests
200g organic crème fraîche
grated plain chocolate,
   to decorate

Peel the pears, leaving the stem attached. In a large heavy-based saucepan combine the wine, cinnamon, cloves, honey and the clementine juice and peel.	**0–10 minutes**
Place the pears in a single layer in the saucepan. Cover the pears with some greaseproof paper and then cover the saucepan. Leave to simmer over a low heat for about 40 minutes, turning occasionally.	**10–20 minutes**
Whiz the onion and garlic in a food processor.	**20–30 minutes**
Heat the oil in a large saucepan and add the onion and garlic. Sauté the onion for about 5 minutes. Add the canned tomatoes, tomato purée, sugar and Italian seasoning. Cook gently over a low heat until the mixture is thickened and reduced.	
Turn the pears.	**30–40 minutes**
For the vinaigrette: Mix the olive oil with the juice of the lemon and some chopped scallion. Taste and season. Deseed and finely chop the chilli and set aside until later.	
Cover the mussels with cold water, discarding any that remain open. Scrub the mussels under cold running water and remove the beards.	
Preheat the oven to 190°C/375°F/Gas Mark 5. Set the plaice fillets in a single layer, skin side down, in a large baking dish. Add just enough water to surround each fillet. Bake the fish in the oven for about 15–20 minutes, depending upon the thickness of the fillets.	
Turn the pears.	**50–60 minutes**
Add the mussels to the tomato sauce. Cover the saucepan with a lid and simmer over a low heat for about 5 minutes (until the mussels are heated through and have opened – discard any that remain closed). Remove the saucepan from the heat but leave the lid on. Remove some of the mussels from the shells.	
Remove the pears from the heat and leave to cool. They taste better cold.	

Bring a large saucepan of lightly salted water to the boil to cook the linguine.

To serve

Slice the bread. Drizzle the vinaigrette over the plaice and serve at the table, garnished with some chopped chillies.

Add the linguine to the saucepan of boiling water, bring back to the boil and cook until the pasta is *al dente*. Drain well and toss with the tomato and mussel sauce. Serve sprinkled with chopped basil and parsley.

Serve each person a poached pear on a meringue nest, topped with a little crème fraîche and a dusting of grated chocolate (very impressive).

...and to drink

Chardonnay Beaujolais Villages

North African Twist

€€

It was Sue Keating who introduced me to adding a little lemon juice to fillet steak. She used to cook the fillet steak under the grill with a little dollop of butter, a drizzle of lemon juice and some salt and pepper. I always remember how tender and succulent the steak was and how the lemon lifted the flavour of the meat juices. If you don't have a grill, a griddle pan will do the job nicely. When I was at college I was addicted to ginger cake and cups of tea. We created this recipe as part of the *Yumee* show and it's so delicious it's now baked on a regular basis. A great excuse to have cups of tea!

Mozzarella salad with a walnut dressing

Grilled fillet steak with cumin- and coriander-roasted carrot and potato

Ginger cake

1 fennel bulb
2 bags mixed salad leaves
   (rocket, watercress
   and/or baby chard)
handful fresh flat-leaf parsley
2 balls mozzarella cheese
12 cherry tomatoes
1 large handful walnuts
   (crumbled by hand)

Dressing
1 tbsp rice wine vinegar
2 tsp lemon juice
1 tsp honey
2 tbsp olive oil
2 tbsp walnut oil

8 carrots
5 potatoes
3 red onions
2 red peppers
5 tbsp extra virgin olive oil
1½ tsp ground cumin
1½ tsp ground coriander
6 x 175g fillet steaks,
   about 3–4cm thick
1 lemon
salt and pepper

180g butter, softened
180g soft light brown sugar
4 eggs
2 tsp ground ginger
1 tsp allspice
1 tsp vanilla extract
350g plain white flour
1 heaped tsp baking powder
220g black treacle
icing sugar, for dusting
whipped cream, to serve

Preheat the oven to 170°C/325°F/Gas Mark 3. Cream the butter and sugar together. Add the eggs one at a time and mix well. Add the ground ginger, allspice and vanilla extract. Mix well.

0–10 minutes

Sift the flour and baking powder into the egg mixture and fold in. Using a wooden spoon mix the treacle into the cake batter until the batter is dark in colour. Grease the bottom of a 25-cm cake tin with a little butter and line the tin with baking paper. Bake in the oven for about 50 minutes.

10–20 minutes

Cut the carrots into thick strips. Peel the potatoes and cut them into thick wedges. Cut the onions into quarters. Cut the peppers into thick strips.

20–30 minutes

Trim and finely slice the fennel bulb. Put the salad leaves, sliced fennel, fennel tops and parsley into a bowl and toss. Tear the mozzarella cheese into thick pieces. Cut the tomatoes in half and add these to the salad.

Heat 2 tablespoons of the olive oil in a large non-stick ovenproof griddle pan. Griddle the carrot, potato, onion and red pepper for about 8 minutes, turning with a spatula.

Mix all the ingredients for the salad dressing together in a jar or whisk together in a bowl.

Take the cake out of the oven and increase the oven temperature to 220°C/425°F/Gas Mark 7.

50–60 minutes

Heat a baking tray in the oven. Transfer the vegetables to the hot baking tray, add the ground coriander, ground cumin and salt and pepper and toss. Put the vegetables in the oven for about 15 minutes.

Add the mozzarella cheese and the dressing to the salad and toss. Sprinkle the walnuts on top. Serve in the centre of the table in a salad bowl.

To serve

Season the steaks on both sides with a little pepper and rub with some olive oil. Heat a griddle pan until white hot. Cook the steaks for about 2–3 minutes on each side for medium-rare. Remove the steaks from the pan and leave to rest on a plate for a few minutes. Drizzle with a little lemon juice and oil. Carve the steaks into thick slices and place on top of the roasted vegetables. Divide the juices between the plates, drizzling them over the meat.

When the cake has cooled, dust with a little icing sugar and serve with whipped cream.

...and to drink   *Montepulciano d'Abruzzo, Valpolicella or Pinot Noir*

Sunday Curry

When I first made this dish my friend Anthony Johns was over for dinner. He raved about my curry so much that I had to circulate the recipe among my friends. Now I share the secret of my curry with you!

€–€€

Aperitif with Bombay mix

Spicy lamb curry with dates, almonds and couscous

Lemon and mango sorbet

1 packet Bombay mix	200g stoned dates
	300ml single cream
2 red onions	500g medium-grain couscous
1 green pepper	600ml warm water
50g flaked almonds	6 plain mini naan breads
4 tbsp sunflower oil	8 plain poppadoms
900g or 5–6 gigot lamb chops, not less than 2.5cm thick, each cut in 3 pieces	natural yoghurt and mango chutney, to serve
1½ heaped tbsp hot Madras curry paste	**1 tub lemon sorbet**
200ml white wine	**1 tub mango sorbet**
1 heaped tbsp mango chutney	**fresh mint leaves, to decorate**

Preheat the oven to 180°C/350°F/Gas Mark 4. Roughly chop the onions and pepper into bite-sized chunks. Dry-fry the almonds in a heavy-based frying pan, until they start to release a scent. This should take about 2 minutes. Remove the almonds from the pan for later use.

0–10 minutes

Heat half the oil in the same pan and brown the lamb on both sides. Remove the meat from the pan and place in a casserole dish. Using the same pan, fry the onions and pepper for about 1 minute. Add the curry paste and mix well.

10–20 minutes

Add the wine and leave to simmer for about 2 minutes. Add the chutney, dates, almonds and cream. Mix well. Pour the sauce over the meat in the casserole dish. Cover the dish, place in the oven and cook for 35–40 minutes.

20–30 minutes

Cook the poppadoms individually in a microwave oven for about 15 seconds on Medium.

30–40 minutes

Place the naan breads on a baking tray. Put the couscous into a heatproof bowl. Add warm water. Stir with a fork so that the water is absorbed evenly. After about 8 minutes add the remaining oil.

40–50 minutes

Use a fork to stir the couscous, to air it and break up any lumps. Cover the dish with foil and set aside ready to go in the oven. Heat the naan breads in the oven for about 8 minutes. Remove the lamb from the oven and leave it to rest for about 5 minutes before serving.

50–60 minutes

Serve the Bombay mix with drinks. Beer is ideal for this meal.

To serve

Reduce the oven temperature to 150°C/300°F/Gas Mark 2 and heat the couscous through. Stir before serving. Heat the plates at the same time. Put the poppadoms and naan breads in baskets and place on the table. Put the lamb in a warmed serving dish and place on the table with some bowls of chutney and yoghurt.

Take the sorbet out of the freezer about 5 minutes before serving. Serve it in chilled bowls with a little mint leaf on top of each, to decorate.

Cobra beer
Very cold Gewürztraminer or Cava, or emphasise the heat with
Shiraz-Cabernet

...and to drink

New Year's Eve Dinner

This dinner is expensive but worth the money for a special occasion. You'll need to allow some extra time to prepare the oysters, unless you have someone to shuck them for you. You may want to make sure you have an oyster shucker and an electric whisk before you attempt the starter and the dessert. You can use rock or native oysters. The main course is straightforward enough. It's one of my brother's specialities. I recommend cooking the duck for 4 minutes, leaving it nice and pink, and giving it time to rest before serving. The mousse has various stages but the effort will be rewarded by the oohs and aahs of your guests as they enjoy the light fluffy lemon tang and find the Champagne raspberries as a surprise at the bottom of the glass. To extend the dinner you could always serve a cheese plate and some chocolates. Shucking oysters is not something I enjoy doing so I cheat here and always get François to do this part, leaving me to concentrate on the mousse.

Aperitif with oysters

Roast duck breast with a honey and ginger sauce, roast sweet potatoes and spinach

Lemon mousse with Champagne raspberries

3 dozen oysters on
   the half shell

2 lemons

6 large boneless Barbary duck
   breasts, about 350g each

½ red chilli, deseeded
   and finely chopped

350g spinach

1 lemon

10 sweet potatoes

2 tbsp olive oil

1 tbsp runny honey

salt and pepper

Honey and ginger sauce

1 tsp grated root ginger

1 tsp Dijon mustard

1 tbsp tomato ketchup

2 tbsp soy sauce

2 tbsp runny honey

2 tbsp medium sherry

150ml chicken stock

170g fresh raspberries,
   plus extra to decorate

300ml double cream

150ml Champagne or
   sparkling white wine

50g caster sugar

juice and grated rind
   of 2 lemons

3 eggs

lemon rind, to decorate

0–10 minutes	Soak the raspberries in the Champagne. Whip the cream until thick. Separate the egg yolks from the whites. Whisk the egg whites until they are stiff.
10–20 minutes	Put the sugar, lemon juice and rind and egg yolks in a heat-resistant bowl set over a saucepan of boiling water. Whisk the mixture until it is light and fluffy and a pale yellow colour (this should take about 3 minutes using a hand-held electric whisk).
20–30 minutes	Using a rubber spatula fold the cream into the lemon mixture, then fold in the egg whites. Put about 3 raspberries into the bottom of a wine glass and then spoon in some mousse. Fill 6 glasses with the mousse. Place the glasses on a tray and leave to set in the refrigerator.
	Peel the sweet potatoes and cut into bite-sized chunks. Put the sweet potato chunks onto a baking tray, drizzle with the oil and season with salt and pepper.
30–40 minutes	Remove the stalks from the spinach. Put all the ingredients for the sauce, except the chicken stock, into a small mixing bowl and set aside for later use. Preheat the oven to 180°C/350°F/Gas Mark 4. With 20 minutes to go put the sweet potatoes in the oven.
	After 10 minutes' cooking take the sweet potatoes out of the oven and drizzle them with the honey. Increase the oven temperature to 220°C/425°F/Gas Mark 7. Put the sweet potatoes in the lower part of the oven and cook for a further 5–8 minutes – watch that they don't get too mushy.

Season both sides of the duck breasts with salt and pepper. Score the fat on the duck breasts by making 3 small slits. Place the duck breasts, skin side down, in a hot, dry frying pan. Cook them over a moderate heat for about 4 minutes. Pour off any excess fat, turn and cook for about a minute to seal the other side. Remove the breasts from the pan and place them in a hot roasting dish, skin side down. Put them in the oven for about 4 minutes for medium-rare, 6 minutes for medium and at least 10 minutes for well done.

Remove the duck breasts from the oven and leave them to rest while you make the sauce.

50–60 minutes

For the sauce: Pour off any fat left in the pan. Add the chicken stock to the pan and allow to boil over a medium heat. Add the remaining ingredients and boil for about 2 minutes to thicken to the consistency of a sauce.

Put the spinach into a steamer. Cook until wilted (about 3 minutes), place in a warmed serving bowl, season with salt and drizzle with a little lemon juice.

Using an oyster shucker and a towel to protect your hands, open the oysters and place them on a large platter. You may need assistance with this but once you get the hang of it you'll have them open in no time. Cut the lemons into quarters and arrange them neatly on the platter. Return the platter to the fridge until you are ready to serve.

To serve

Serve each person 6 oysters. They taste great with just a small squeeze of lemon. If you fancy something with a little more spice try them with a drop of Tabasco sauce.

Thinly slice the duck breasts and arrange on warmed plates. Pour over a little sauce and serve at once. Put the sweet potatoes and the spinach in serving bowls and place on the table.

Decorate the top of each mousse with a raspberry and a swirl of lemon rind, and serve.

Champagne
Bordeaux or Burgundy

...and to drink

Family Lunch

€€

This is a light and easy meal to prepare. The soup is wholesome and warming and the salmon is full of nutrients. Although this is a simple meal it's Joan's sauce that really makes it special. (Joan is the mother of Sue Keating.) My mum made this sauce for the first time many years ago, and I got addicted to it instantly. The measurements in the ingredients are just a guideline. You can add more or less of what you like so that it suits your taste buds. Joan's sauce is ideal with cold or hot salmon and for a light meal. If you fancy cutting back on some of the calories there is no need to add butter to the potatoes and peas.

Mushroom soup

Baked salmon with Joan's sauce, served with baby potatoes and peas

Vanilla ice cream with a berry coulis and a vanilla shortbread biscuit

2 tbsp olive oil

1 large onion, roughly chopped

1 large potato, peeled
   and chopped

1kg button mushrooms

150ml sherry

1 organic vegetable stock cube

2 bay leaves

salt and pepper

single cream and chopped
   fresh parsley, to garnish

sliced brown bread and
   butter, to serve

6 salmon fillets

4 tbsp olive oil

1kg baby potatoes

450g frozen peas

salt and pepper

lemon wedges, snipped
   fresh chives and chopped
   fresh parsley, to garnish

Joan's sauce

2 large tbsp mayonnaise

200g crème fraîche

50–100ml single cream

2–3 drops Worcestershire

sauce

2–3 drops tomato ketchup

¼ tsp mild curry powder

a squeeze of lemon juice

400g frozen berries

1–2 tbsp lemon juice

1 heaped tbsp icing sugar

**1 tub good quality
   vanilla ice cream**

**vanilla shortbread
   biscuits, to serve**

0–10 minutes

Heat the oil in a large saucepan. Fry the onions until they are transparent, then add the potatoes, stirring occasionally. Cook for a further 2 minutes. Wipe the mushrooms clean. Add the whole mushrooms, including the stalks, to the saucepan. Stir once or twice, then add the sherry and cook for a further 2 minutes, stirring occasionally.

10–20 minutes

Sprinkle the stock cube over the mushrooms and add 850ml hot water. Add 2 bay leaves. Season with salt and pepper, cover the saucepan and simmer for about 25 minutes

20–30 minutes

Preheat the oven to 250°C/475°F/Gas Mark 9.

Scale the salmon and remove any large bones. Line a baking tray with foil. Put the fillets, skin side down, on the foil. Brush with oil and season with salt and pepper.

30–40 minutes

For the sauce: Combine the mayonnaise and crème fraîche in a bowl. Thin the mixture by adding some cream and a little lemon juice, then mix in the rest of the ingredients. Add more cream or lemon juice to taste. Set aside in the fridge until you are ready to serve.

Bring a saucepan of lightly salted water to the boil. Put the potatoes in a steamer set over the saucepan of boiling water.

Put the salmon in the oven and roast for 20–25 minutes.

40–50 minutes

Remove the soup from the heat. Take out the bay leaves and discard, and blend the soup using a hand-held blender. Return the soup to a very low heat, just warming it through until you are ready to serve.

50–60 minutes

Purée the berries with the lemon juice and sugar in a food processor. Strain by pressing through a large non-metallic sieve, using the back of a spoon. Chill in the fridge.

Bring a saucepan of lightly salted water to the boil. Follow the packet instructions for cooking the peas – it should take 3 minutes.

Ladle the soup into bowls, garnish with a drizzle of cream and some parsley and serve with sliced brown bread and butter.

Remove the salmon from the oven and transfer to a warmed serving dish. Put the potatoes in a serving dish and garnish with lemon, chives and parsley. Drain the peas and toss them in a little butter.

A couple of minutes before serving remove the ice cream from the freezer. Serve each person a portion of ice cream drizzled with coulis, with a shortbread biscuit on the side.

To serve

White Burgundy, Australian Riesling or Pinot Noir

...and to drink

Game Season Feast

One of the first meals François made for me was wood pigeon cooked in cider. Later on he informed me that he had found the pigeon on the road. I still can't believe to this day that he cooked it and I ate it. Now I don't expect you to use 'road kill' but his recipe works very well with pheasant. Get wild pheasants, if you can. The bresaola should be very thinly sliced from a large piece, if possible, but it is also available pre-sliced.

€€–€€€

Bresaola with rocket

Pheasant casseroled in cider with roast potato wedges

Poached pears in honey and cardamom

24 thin slices bresaola	3 red onions, roughly chopped	**6 good-sized pears**
75g block Parmesan cheese	1 garlic clove, chopped	**400ml water**
handful rocket leaves	4–5 tbsp olive oil	**3 large tbsp runny honey**
extra virgin olive oil,	2 pheasants, about 675g each	**8–10 cardamom pods**
for drizzling	500ml cider	**fresh mint leaves, to decorate**
1 lemon	3 tbsp mango chutney	**1 tub good quality vanilla**
	1 large handful raisins	**ice cream, to serve**
	1.5kg potatoes	
	olive oil	
	salt and pepper	

Using a vegetable peeler, thinly peel the pears, retaining the stem, if possible. Bring the water to a simmer in a large saucepan. Add the honey and the cardamom pods. Stir. Carefully place the pears in the saucepan. Lay a piece of baking paper on top of the pears and then cover the saucepan. Cook over a low heat for about 35 minutes.

0–10 minutes

Divide the bresaola between 6 plates. Using a vegetable peeler, shave off thin slices of the cheese.

10–20 minutes

20–30 minutes	Turn the pears.
	Heat 2–3 tablespoons of the oil in a large heavy-based casserole dish. Add the onion and garlic and soften.
30–40 minutes	Turn the pears.
	Add the pheasants to the casserole dish and toss them with the onions and garlic for about 2 minutes, browning them slightly. Add the cider and cook for about 3 minutes, then add the chutney and raisins and season with a little salt and pepper. Cover and cook over a low heat for about 30 minutes.
	Remove the pears from the heat.
40–50 minutes	Preheat the oven to 200°C/400°F/Gas Mark 6. Cut the potatoes into quarters, leaving the skin on. Using your fingers, toss the potatoes wedges in about 2 tablespoons of oil and season with salt and pepper. Arrange the potato wedges on a baking tray, place in the oven and cook for about 25 minutes.
50–60 minutes	Remove the pheasants from the casserole dish and set aside, leaving the sauce to cook over a low heat for a further 5 minutes.
To serve	Scatter some of the cheese shavings over each plate of bresaola. Add some rocket, drizzle with oil and a drop of lemon juice and serve.
	Carve the pheasants, set the pieces of meat on a warmed serving platter and drizzle over the sauce. Serve warm, with the potatoes straight from the oven.
	Warm the pears slightly before serving. Serve each person a pear with some lovely sauce and a scoop of ice cream, decorated with a fresh mint leaf.
...and to drink	*Côtes du Rhône or Grand Cru St-Emilion*

The Best Fish Dish

My grandmother had this terrific method of cooking fish. No matter what fish it was she would bake it whole smothered in tomatoes and fennel. The fish was always cooked perfectly and came away from the bone so easily. I have adapted her method and used whole sea bass. Not only will the flavours linger, the dish has a definite wow factor.

€€

Lemon and herb salad with creamy goat's cheese croûtons

Baked whole sea bass with fennel and tomatoes

Amaretti crunch ice cream with a mango coulis

125g soft goat's cheese
  (Cabridoux)
1 small shallot, finely chopped
2 tbsp finely chopped tarragon
1–2 tbsp single cream
2 heads lettuce
pine kernels, for sprinkling

Dressing
5 tbsp olive oil
2–3 tbsp fresh lemon juice
finely chopped fresh parsley,
  tarragon and chives
salt and pepper

3 fennel bulbs
500g fresh vine-ripened
  tomatoes
1 tbsp olive oil
2 onions, sliced
1 garlic clove, crushed
200ml white wine
juice of ½ lime
400g canned chopped
  organic tomatoes
2–3 whole sea bass,
  960g–1kg in total
2 tbsp olive oil
450g long-grain rice

salt and pepper
fresh flat-leaf parsley,
  to garnish

**2 ripe mangoes, peeled
  and stoned**
caster sugar, to taste
**1 tub good quality
  vanilla ice cream**
**1 packet Amaretti biscuits
  (crunchy variety)**

Preheat the oven to 190°C/375°F/Gas Mark 5. Slice the fennel. Cut the tomatoes into chunks. Heat some oil in a large casserole dish. Sweat the onions for about 2 minutes. Add the chopped tomatoes, fennel and garlic.

0–10 minutes

10–20 minutes Toss the tomatoes, fennel and garlic with the onions. Add the white wine and lime juice and cook for 1 minute. Add the canned tomatoes, season with salt and pepper, stir and remove from the heat. Using a sharp knife scale the sea bass, holding the tail firmly and scraping the knife along the outside of the fish. Do this in the kitchen sink as the scales tend to fly everywhere. Remove the heads from the fish, if you prefer.

20–30 minutes Beat the goat's cheese with the shallot and tarragon and add a little cream to thin the mixture slightly. Mix the dressing ingredients together. Taste and season with salt and pepper.

Put the pine kernels on a baking tray and place them in the oven for about 5 minutes.

30–40 minutes Whiz the mangoes in a food processor until runny. If not sweet enough add a little caster sugar and whiz again. Set in the fridge to chill.

Remove the pine kernels from the oven.

40–50 minutes Pour about half of the tomato mixture into the base of a large deep baking dish. Lay the whole fish on top. Cover with the rest of the tomato mixture. Cover the dish with foil and place in the oven for about 15–20 minutes.

Put a large saucepan of lightly salted water on to boil.

50–60 minutes Put the rice in the boiling water and cook until it is *al dente*. Slice the French stick into thick slices. Drizzle a little oil over the base of a baking dish and toss the slices of bread in the oil. Place the dish in the top part of the oven for about 8 minutes to brown the bread.

When the rice is cooked, drain it through a sieve and then put it into an ovenproof bowl. Add a little oil, fluff with a fork and cover with foil. Take the toasted bread out of the oven.

To serve Dress and toss the salad, sprinkling the toasted pine kernels on top. Put a dollop of goat's cheese mixture on each crispy piece of bread and arrange the bread on top of the salad.

Put the rice in the oven for 5 minutes. Let the sea bass rest for a minute before serving. Sprinkle some freshly chopped parsley on top. Serve the baked sea bass and the rice at the table – warn your guests to watch out for bones.

Put a scoop of ice cream in each of 6 bowls, crumble the Amaretti biscuits on top and then drizzle with the mango coulis.

...and to drink   *Delicate Chablis*

Winter in the Med

Ratatouille can be served with many meats and fish. A definite staple in my home, this recipe can be made any time of the year. When picking a striploin steak make sure it's slightly marbled as the fat gives the meat delicious flavour.

€€

Baked goat's cheese in a walnut crust on a bed of herb salad with walnut dressing

Striploin steak with ratatouille

Baked apples with sweet walnuts

2 slices brown bread

handful walnuts

600g sliced goat's cheese

2 tbsp walnut oil

2 bags mixed salad leaves,
    including rocket,
    red chard, baby leaf
    spinach and mustard

Dressing

1 tsp Dijon mustard

2 tbsp white wine vinegar

1 tsp maple syrup

4 tbsp walnut oil

2 tbsp olive oil

salt and pepper

1 garlic clove

6 x 175g striploin steaks

3 tbsp olive oil

sea salt

freshly cracked black pepper

Ratatouille

2 red onions

4 courgettes

6 vine-ripened tomatoes

2 garlic cloves

2 tbsp olive oil

400g canned chopped
    tomatoes

1 tbsp tomato purée

1 tsp sugar

1 tsp oregano

1 bay leaf

salt and pepper

6 large eating apples

2 tbsp chopped walnuts

2 tbsp raisins

1 tsp cinnamon

2 tbsp soft light brown sugar

2 tbsp maple syrup

25g butter

4 tbsp water

pouring cream, to serve

Cut a clove of garlic in half and rub each side of the steaks with it. Rub the steaks with a little olive oil and sprinkle with cracked black pepper. Set aside.

For the ratatouille: Roughly chop the onions. Chop the courgettes into bite-sized chunks and roughly chop the tomatoes. Finely chop the garlic or crush in a garlic press.

0–10 minutes

Put the oil in a large heavy-based saucepan and sauté the onion and garlic. Add the courgettes. Stir and cook for a further 2 minutes. Add the chopped tomatoes, canned tomatoes and tomato purée. Stir well. Add the sugar, oregano and the bay leaf and season with salt and pepper. Reduce the heat and cover the saucepan. Simmer the ratatouille for 30 minutes.

10–20 minutes

Preheat the oven to 180°C/375°F/Gas Mark 4.

Core the apples. Cut the base of each apple so that they can sit upright in a baking dish. Mix the walnuts, raisins, cinnamon and brown sugar in a bowl. Stuff the apples with the sugar and nut filling and put a little knob of butter on each apple. Put the apples into a baking dish with the water. Drizzle each apple with a little maple syrup. Cover the baking dish with foil. Put the dish in the oven and bake the apples for about 35 minutes.

20–30 minutes

For the dressing: Dissolve the mustard in the vinegar. Add the maple syrup and whisk in the walnut oil and the olive oil, adding a little at a time. Taste as you go – you may prefer less oil. Season with salt and pepper.

30–40 minutes

In a food processor whiz the brown bread and the walnuts until they have been reduced to coarse crumbs. Put the crumbs on a large plate.

Put some walnut oil in a small saucer. Dip each slice of goat's cheese in the walnut oil and then in the crumbs. Coat each side of the cheese with a layer of crumbs. Place each piece in a baking dish.

40–50 minutes

Turn off the heat under the ratatouille. Leave the lid on so the heat is retained and the flavours have time to rest. Don't remove the lid until just before serving.

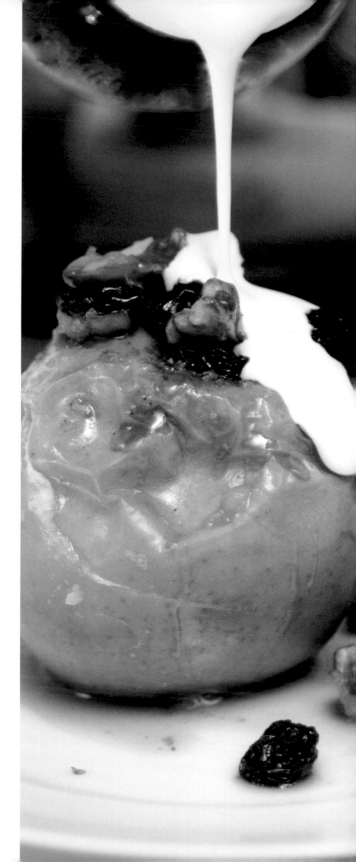

50–60 minutes Put the cheese in the oven and bake for about 8 minutes. The cheese should be slightly melted on the outside and the crumb crust should be crisp. Serve immediately. Toss the salad leaves in the dressing.

To serve Place a handful of dressed salad leaves in the centre of each plate and set the baked goat's cheese on top.

Turn off the oven but leave the apples to rest in the oven so they keep warm.

Ask your guests how they like their meat cooked. Heat the griddle pan, season the steaks with a little sea salt and place the steaks on the hot pan. Allow 2 minutes each side for rare, 3 minutes each side for medium-rare, 4 minutes each side for medium and 5–6 minutes each side for well done. Rest the steaks on a side plate before serving.

Serve each person a baked apple with some pouring cream on the side.

...and to drink *Light fresh Sauvignon, to start Shiraz/Syrah*

Spring

Oriental Flair

€–€€

At first glance it may seem that a lot of ingredients are required for the chicken dish. Don't get stressed! Once the ingredients have been prepared they all go in the same baking dish, leaving fewer dishes to wash! The peach pudding is my mother's recipe. It was her way of giving us a little bit of summer in cold, rainy Ireland.

Orange ginger chicken with cashew nuts and rice

Warm peach pudding with vanilla cream

2 garlic cloves

2 tbsp finely grated root ginger

4 tbsp runny honey

3 tbsp soy sauce

grated rind and juice of 1 large orange

juice of 1 lemon

6 boned free-range chicken breasts, skin on

2 tbsp sunflower oil

2 handfuls cashew nuts

500g easy-cook mixed long-grain and wild rice

2 bunches scallions (spring onions)

1 red pepper

300g baby button mushrooms

pepper

120g margarine

120g caster sugar

1 tsp vanilla extract

2 eggs

240g self-raising flour

3–4 tbsp water

675g canned peach slices
   in natural juice

Vanilla cream

300ml cream

½ tsp vanilla extract

1 tsp sugar

0–10 minutes

Preheat the oven to 190°C/375°F/Gas Mark 5.

Cream the margarine and sugar together, add the vanilla extract, beat in the eggs and stir in the flour and water. (This can all be done in a food processor.)

10–20 minutes

Strain the peaches through a non-metallic sieve. Layer the peach slices in the base of a 25-cm pie dish. Spoon the sponge mixture over the top and smooth it out with the back of a metal spoon. Dip the spoon in a cup of hot water to make it easier to spread the mixture. Place in the bottom half of the oven and bake for about 45–50 minutes.

In a food processor whiz the garlic, ginger, honey, soy sauce, orange rind and juice and lemon juice together. Trim any excess fat from the chicken.

20–30 minutes

Heat the oil in a frying pan and cook the chicken, skin side down, for about 3 minutes on each side, until golden brown. When browned, transfer the chicken to an ovenproof dish, skin side up. Pour the sauce over the chicken, season with pepper and scatter the cashew nuts on top. Place in the oven and bake for about 15 minutes.

30–40 minutes

Bring a large saucepan of lightly salted water to the boil. Place the rice in a sieve and rinse well under cold running water. Add the rice to the boiling water and return to the boil. Stir once, cover, reduce the heat and simmer for about 18 minutes or until the rice is tender.

40–50 minutes

Trim the scallions and slice diagonally. Deseed the red pepper and slice diagonally. Wipe the baby button mushrooms clean using some damp kitchen paper.

After 15 minutes remove the chicken from the oven, add the scallions, red pepper and mushrooms, then baste the chicken with the sauce, return to the oven and bake for a further 10 minutes.

50–60 minutes

Put a kettle of water on to boil.

When the rice is tender, drain through a sieve and rinse through with boiling water.

Remove the pudding from the oven.

Serve each person a portion of rice and a chicken breast, skin side up, sitting on some of the vegetables. Make sure to give everyone plenty of the wonderful juices.

To serve

Whip the cream, vanilla extract and sugar together until you achieve the consistency of thick pouring cream. The pudding should be served slightly warm with the vanilla cream around the sides.

White Burgundy

...and to drink

Cooking with Kids

This is an ideal lunch menu and can easily be adapted to serve a large group. To make this meal really special invest in the first course. Find a really great deli that has a good range of Italian and Spanish imports. Farmers' markets generally have a fantastic selection. At first sight the cannelloni has lots of annoying fiddly bits, but once you get the hang of it I guarantee it will become a staple dinner dish. Having made cannelloni with mum since I was a child I have yet to discover a tidy way to make it. Stuffing the tubes is a messy job so just get on with it and then clean up when done. Or, better still, get the kids involved and have them do the stuffing.

€–€€

Italian antipasti

Ricotta and spinach cannelloni

Crisp garden salad

Vanilla ice cream with a sweet raspberry sauce

12 very thin slices
   prosciutto crudo
12 slices salami
olives
caperberries
marinated grilled peppers
ready-to-bake ciabatta bread

300g spinach
500g ricotta cheese
4 tbsp grated Parmesan cheese
freshly grated nutmeg
juice of 1 lemon

250g pre-cooked
   cannelloni tubes
salt and pepper

Sauce

25g white Cheddar cheese
25g butter
25g flour
600ml milk
1 onion, finely chopped
400g canned chopped
   tomatoes
2 tbsp tomato purée

50ml red wine
1 tsp sugar
2 garlic cloves, crushed
2 tbsp chopped fresh oregano
2 tbsp chopped fresh basil

2 heads lettuce (different types)
1 small red onion, thinly sliced

Dressing

4 tbsp extra virgin olive oil
2 tbsp rapeseed oil

(Continued on next page...)

2 tbsp red wine vinegar	300g frozen raspberries,	good quality vanilla ice cream
1 tsp Dijon mustard	defrosted	
1 tsp runny honey	juice of 1 lemon	
salt and pepper	4 tbsp icing sugar	

0–10 minutes

For the sauce: Grate the cheese. Melt the butter in a heavy-based saucepan. Add the flour and, using a whisk, stir constantly to combine the flour with the butter. Cook for 1 minute over a low heat, stirring constantly. Add 200ml milk and, using a balloon whisk, stir constantly over a low heat, allowing the sauce to thicken. Continue adding milk until you have a thick sauce.

10–20 minutes

Remove the sauce from the heat, add the cheese and stir. Heat a little oil in a saucepan and sweat the onion. Add the canned tomatoes, tomato purée, wine, 50ml water, the sugar and the garlic. Stir and leave to cook over a low heat.

20–30 minutes

Bring a large saucepan of water to the boil. Wash the spinach. Pour the boiling water into a large heatproof bowl. Drop in the spinach for a second and then drain. Fill a large bowl with cold water and refresh the spinach in the cold water. Mix the ricotta cheese, spinach and 2 tablespoons of the Parmesan cheese together in a bowl. Season with a little freshly grated nutmeg and salt and pepper and add lemon juice, to taste.

30–40 minutes

Add the oregano and basil to the tomato sauce and then pour the sauce into the base of an ovenproof dish. Stuff the cannelloni tubes with the ricotta and spinach mixture. Place each roll side by side in a single layer.

Preheat the oven to 190°C/375°F/Gas Mark 5.

40–50 minutes

Pour the cheese sauce over the cannelloni. Sprinkle with the remaining Parmesan cheese and transfer to the oven for about 35 minutes.

Mix all the dressing ingredients together in a jar.

50–60 minutes

Put the bread in the oven. Arrange all the antipasti on a large serving plate.

Place the antipasti in the centre of the table and allow your guests to serve themselves from the plate. Serve the ciabatta warm from the oven.

Leave the cannelloni to sit for about 5 minutes before serving.

Dress and toss the salad and serve with the cannelloni.

Press the raspberries through a non-metallic sieve into a bowl. Add lemon juice and icing sugar to taste. Divide the ice cream between 6 individual serving bowls, spoon over the sauce and serve.

Valpolicella   **...and to drink**

Indian Feast

€–€€

This is a very easy dish to prepare, so it's great for the beginner cook. Buy readymade poppadoms or get some in from your local Indian takeaway. But do make the naan breads yourself as the smell of these cooking will really impress your guests.

Chicken korma with homemade naan breads, served with chutney and a cucumber and red onion salsa

Fresh pineapple

2 tbsp sunflower oil

2 onions

2 tsp hot chilli powder

2 tsp ground turmeric

50g flaked almonds

230ml double cream

500g organic natural yoghurt

3 garlic cloves

100g ground almonds

2 handfuls sultanas

675g or 6 boneless free-
    range chicken breasts

salt and pepper

finely chopped fresh
    coriander, to garnish

To serve

3 x 125g bags mixed long-grain
    and wild boil-in-the-bag rice

poppadoms

green label mango chutney

Cucumber and red onion salsa

2 red onions, finely chopped

½ cucumber, peeled and
    finely chopped

handful fresh coriander,
    finely chopped

Naan breads

2 tsp dried yeast

150ml warm milk

2 heaped tsp granulated sugar

½ tsp salt

1 tsp baking powder

150ml natural yoghurt

2 tbsp sunflower oil

450g strong white flour

juice of 1 orange

**1 large pineapple, skin
    and eyes removed,
    cut into thick slices**

0–10 minutes

For the naan breads: Put the yeast into a large mixing bowl. Add the milk and mix well to make sure the yeast is dissolved. Add the sugar, salt, baking powder, yoghurt and oil. Add the flour a cup at a time and mix with your hands. Form a dough ball. Remove the dough from the bowl and knead on a large work surface. (All of this can be done in a food mixer.)

10–20 minutes	Put the dough ball in a bowl, cover with clingfilm and set aside in a warm part of the kitchen or in the hot press to rise. This should take 50–60 minutes.
	Preheat the oven to 200°C/400°F/Gas Mark 6.
	Heat the oil in a frying pan. Finely chop the onions, add to the pan and cook for about 3 minutes until soft. Add the hot chilli powder and turmeric to the onion and mix gently. Remove the onion from the heat and allow the spices to be absorbed by the onion.
	Put the flaked almonds on a baking tray and toast in the oven.
20–30 minutes	Put the onion, cream, yoghurt, garlic, ground almonds and one handful of the sultanas in a food processor and whiz. Season with a pinch of salt and pepper. Whiz until well blended.
	Cut each chicken breast into about 6 pieces. Grease a casserole dish with 1 tablespoon of the oil. Place the chicken pieces in the dish and cover with the sauce. Add the remainder of the sultanas and the toasted almonds. Mix well, coating all the chicken with the sauce. Bake in the oven for about 30–35 minutes.
30–40 minutes	*For the salsa*: Mix the onion, cucumber and coriander together.
	Cut the pineapple into bite-sized chunks, toss in the orange juice and place in the fridge.
40–50 minutes	Bring a large saucepan of water to the boil. Carefully place the rice bags in the saucepan (1 bag for 2 people) and add salt, if required. Cover and simmer for 20 minutes.
50–60 minutes	By now the bread should have risen. Knock it back and then knead again for about 5 minutes. Break off little dough rolls and flatten them with the palm of your hand. Set them out on a large tray.
	Remove the chicken from the oven and garnish with the chopped coriander.

Place an empty baking tray in the oven and allow it to heat. When the tray is hot, toss the flattened dough onto the tray, return to the oven and bake for about 6–8 minutes.

To serve

Put the poppadoms, chutney and salsa on the table. Drain the rice. Put some rice on each plate and place the chicken on the table in the casserole dish. Allow your guests to serve themselves. Put the naan breads, straight from the oven, in a basket lined with a tea towel to keep them warm, and place on the table.

Serve the pineapple straight from the fridge.

Australian Riesling **...and to drink**

Asian Fusion

The trick to stir-frying is to have all the ingredients deseeded, chopped, sliced and ready to go before you even start to think about cooking anything. This type of dinner is ideal if you plan to eat around your kitchen table. As your guests chow down on the delicate and tasty fish cakes you can show off your cooking skills while stir-frying the pork. Bash the wok a little more and the sounds, smells and final display of the dish will make even an amateur cook seem expert.

€–€€

Asian-style fish cakes with dipping sauce

Stir-fried pork with mixed vegetables and oyster sauce

Fresh fruit

1 red chilli	**Dipping sauce**	350g tender stem broccoli
2 limes	1 red chilli	3 garlic cloves
1 stalk lemon grass	2 garlic cloves, crushed	25g root ginger
1 garlic clove	4 tbsp lime juice	450g boneless pork loin chops
3 tbsp fresh coriander	4 tbsp Thai fish sauce	3 tbsp sunflower oil
1 tbsp grated root ginger	3 tbsp light brown sugar	6 tbsp oyster sauce
2 tsp sugar	4 tbsp warm water	1 tbsp runny honey
500g white fish fillets	sliced red chillies, to garnish	1 scallion (spring onion),
(cod or hake)		sliced, to garnish
fresh coriander leaves and	2 onions	750g egg noodles, to serve
wedges of lime, to garnish	3 carrots	
	2 red peppers	**selection of fresh fruit**

Deseed the chilli. Grate the zest of one lime. Put the lemon grass, garlic, coriander, ginger, sugar, lime zest and red chilli into a food processor and whiz to make a paste.

0–10 minutes

10–20 minutes	Add the fish and lightly whiz, just enough to break up the fish. Don't overdo it – you don't want the fish mixture to become a complete mush. Brush the insides of a bun tin with a little sunflower oil. Form the fish mixture into small balls and place them in the individual holes.
20–30 minutes	Finely slice the onions. Slice the carrots into thin strips. Deseed the red pepper and finely slice into strips. Cut the broccoli florets off the stem and then slice the stems into thin strips.
30–40 minutes	*For the dipping sauce*: Deseed the chilli and finely slice into thin rounds. Combine all the sauce ingredients in a jar. Taste and add more sugar if you like.
40–50 minutes	Put the fish cakes in the oven and cook for about 12–15 minutes.
	Remove any fat from the pork and finely slice the meat into thin strips. Finely chop 2 garlic cloves. Peel the ginger and finely chop.
50–60 minutes	Bring a large saucepan of water to the boil for soaking the noodles.
	Heat the oil in a wok over a high heat until smoking. Add the ginger and chopped garlic and fry for a couple of seconds. Quickly add the pork and continue to fry until just cooked through, about 2–3 minutes. Then add the onion, carrots, red peppers and broccoli. Cook for about 3–4 minutes. Add the oyster sauce and the honey. Grate the remaining garlic clove and add this to the pork. Taste and adjust the seasoning as required. Remove from the heat and garnish with some sliced scallion.
To serve	Put 3 fish balls on each of 6 plates and garnish with fresh coriander leaves and a small wedge of lime. Sprinkle a couple of chilli slices over the dipping sauce and serve.
	Soak the noodles in the hot water for about 2–3 minutes. Drain and place in a large serving bowl. Spoon the pork on top of the noodles, garnish with some fresh parsley and serve immediately. Serve with bowls and chopsticks.
	Put a big bowl of fresh fruit on the table so your guests can help themselves.
...and to drink	*Australian Chardonnay*

Mexican Fiesta with Margaritas

I love Mexican food. This is one of my favourite dinners in the book so I hope you enjoy a taste of Mexico. My Aunt Linda is renowned in southern California for her classic margaritas. Homemade salsa will always beat shop bought and it's worth the effort.

Tortilla chips with homemade salsa

Steak fajitas with guacamole, soured cream and salsa

Aunt Linda's golden Californian classic margaritas

1–2 bags crispy tortilla chips

Salsa
8 vine-ripened tomatoes,
    chopped into small chunks
2 red onions, finely chopped
4 tbsp chopped fresh coriander
1–2 tsp sugar
juice of ½ lime
1–2 tsp dried chillies
salt and pepper

1kg sirloin steak
2 red peppers
1 green pepper
2 onions
400g canned red kidney beans

100g white Cheddar
    cheese, grated
18 soft tortilla wraps
lime juice, for drizzling
chopped fresh coriander,
    to garnish

To serve
sliced jalapeño peppers
soured cream or crème fraîche,
1 head Iceberg (Webbs)
    lettuce, shredded

Marinade
2 tbsp sunflower oil
1 tbsp ground cumin
1 tbsp ground coriander
1 tsp crushed dried chillies

Guacamole
1 large vine-ripened tomato
2 ripe avocados
½ red onion
1 tbsp chopped fresh coriander
juice of ½ lime
salt and pepper

70ml tequila
70ml orange liqueur
225ml freshly squeezed
    lime juice
6–8 tbsp caster sugar
a good number of ice cubes
small slices of lime, to decorate
slices of lime and salt, to
    frost the glasses

0–10 minutes	Wrap the steak in clingfilm, place a towel over the top and bash it with either a rolling pin or a meat mallet. This will flatten the steak and tenderise it. Thinly slice the steak into strips.
	For the marinade: Gently heat the sunflower oil in a frying pan. Add the ground cumin, ground coriander and crushed chillies. Heat gently for a second or two. They are ready when you get a spicy scent.
10–20 minutes	Place the strips of steak in a bowl and pour over the marinade. Using your hands, coat the steak with the marinade. Cover with clingfilm and place in the fridge until later.
20–30 minutes	*For the salsa*: In a large bowl mix the chopped tomatoes, onion, coriander, lime juice, sugar and crushed chillies together. Taste and season with a little salt and pepper. Don't be too disappointed if it is not hot enough. Time will bring out all the flavours. Cover with clingfilm and set aside in the fridge.
30–40 minutes	*For the guacamole*: Deseed the tomato (you can add the pulp to the salsa). Roughly chop the onion. Halve, stone and peel the avocados. Using a food processor whiz the tomato, onion, coriander, avocados and lime juice together. Season to taste with salt and pepper. Cover with clingfilm and put in the fridge to chill.
40–50 minutes	Preheat the oven to 180°C/350°F/Gas Mark 4.
	Deseed and finely slice the peppers. Thinly slice the onions. Drain the kidney beans and place them in an ovenproof dish. Scatter with some grated cheese and cover with foil. Wrap all the tortillas in foil. Put the beans in the oven for about 8 minutes.
50–60 minutes	When the beans have been heated reduce the oven temperature to 150°C/300°F/Gas Mark 2 and put the tortillas in the oven.
	Heat a large heavy-based frying pan. Add the marinated steak, onions and peppers. Stir with a spatula and cook until the steak is browned. Just before removing it from the heat, drizzle with a little lime juice and garnish with some fresh coriander.

Put some of the salsa in a bowl and serve with the tortilla chips.

Put the remaining salsa, the soured cream, guacamole, lettuce, jalapeño peppers and grated cheese on the table.

Remove the beans and the tortillas from the oven. Bring the sizzling pan to the table and allow your guests to make their own fajitas. All the passing of bowls is guaranteed to generate a lively atmosphere.

Put all the margarita ingredients into a blender and whiz. The ice should turn into a slushy mixture. Sweeten as you go – if you want extra sugar feel free to add some.

Run a slice of lime around the rim of each glass and then dip the glass in a shallow saucer of salt.

Pour the slushy cocktail into glasses and garnish with small slices of lime. Add a little orange juice to sweeten, if you like.

Family Sunday Lunch

€€ The little tartlets are fun to make with children. Use different toppings and add a few anchovies for a sophisticated approach. The apricot sauce uses dried apricots and needs a little forward planning.

Warm tomato tartlets

Plaice with herb butter and almond green beans

Vanilla ice cream with apricot sauce

425g frozen puff pastry (2 sheets)	100g butter	30g butter
3 large tomatoes, sliced	4 tbsp finely chopped parsley	1 small onion
250g buffalo mozzarella cheese	3–4 tbsp plain flour	150ml single cream
salt and pepper	6 thin fillets of plaice	salt and pepper
5 tbsp good quality pesto and some fresh basil, to garnish	4 tbsp olive oil	
dressed salad leaves, to serve	2 lemons, cut into wedges, to serve	120g dried apricots, soaked overnight
		120g canned apricots
	Almond green beans	600ml water
	20g flaked almonds	1 tub vanilla ice cream
	450g green beans	

0–10 minutes Put 60g butter in a bowl and beat until soft. Add the parsley and a pinch of salt. Scoop the butter into a piece of greaseproof paper. Fold the paper tightly and roll into a sausage shape. Place this in the fridge to harden.

10–20 minutes Put the soaked apricots and the canned apricots into a saucepan with the water. Bring to the boil, then reduce the heat and simmer for about 10 minutes until the liquid has reduced.

20–30 minutes   Liquidise the apricots and press them through a non-metallic sieve. If the sauce is too thin, reduce it by boiling. If it is too thick, add a little water.

Preheat the oven to 200°C/400°F/Gas Mark 6.

Line a baking sheet with baking paper. Roll out the pastry to about the thickness of the edge of a wooden spoon.

30–40 minutes   Using a pastry cutter cut out as many round pastry shapes as you can and place them on the lined baking sheet.

Place the almonds on a baking tray and toast in the oven.

Beat the egg and paint each pastry circle with a little egg wash. Put a slice of tomato onto each pastry circle, then add a slice of mozzarella cheese. Season with salt and pepper.

Remove the almonds from the oven.   **40–50 minutes**

Put the flour on a plate and season with salt and pepper. Run your fingers over the fish to check for bones. Dip each fillet in the flour and shake off any excess. Put the fillets on a clean plate.

Put the tartlets in the oven and bake for about 8–10 minutes, until the pastry is golden   **50–60 minutes**
brown and the cheese has melted. Let them cool slightly but do serve them warm. Garnish with a drizzle of pesto and some fresh basil.

Top and tail the green beans. Bring a large saucepan of lightly salted water to the boil. Add the beans and cook for about 5 minutes. Drain the beans.

In a separate saucepan melt the butter, add the onion and sauté. Add the cream and almonds and bring to the boil. When thickened toss the beans in the sauce. Season with salt and pepper.

Serve the tartlets slightly warm with some dressed salad leaves.   **To serve**

Heat the oil and the remaining butter in 2 frying pans until it starts to bubble. Add the fish and fry for about 3–4 minutes each side. Remove the butter log from the fridge and cut into slices. Put a piece of fish on each of 6 plates and top with a slice of parsley butter. Serve with lemon wedges.

Reheat the apricot sauce and serve it over the ice cream.

White Burgundy   **...and to drink**

Everyday Light Supper

The little lemon pots are fun and novel and will go down a treat after a light meal. This makes an ideal lunch and would even impress the mother-in-law.

€

Smoked pancetta and leek quiche

Garden herb salad

Lemon and raspberry cream pots

6 slices smoked pancetta or smoked streaky bacon	2 heads lettuce (different types)	(You will need 12 small shot glasses)
2 leeks	**Dressing**	400ml cream
225g ready-rolled shortcrust pastry (1 sheet)	6 tbsp extra virgin olive oil	3 tbsp lemon curd
25g white Cheddar cheese	2 tbsp white wine vinegar	150g frozen raspberries, defrosted
5 eggs	1 small garlic clove, crushed	icing sugar, to taste
2 tbsp milk	finely chopped fresh parsley, thyme and mint	grated plain and white chocolate, for decorating
salt and pepper	salt and pepper	

Fry the pancetta in a non-stick frying pan until crisp. Cut the leeks in half and then cut into small rounds.

0–10 minutes

Preheat the oven to 180°C/375°F/Gas Mark 4.

Line a flan dish with the pastry. Gently press down all the edges and cut away any excess, but leave it loose as the pastry will shrink when cooked. Line the pastry with baking paper and baking beans. Place in the oven and bake for about 10 minutes.

Grate the cheese. Remove the pancetta from the pan, blot on kitchen paper and drain off all the fat from the pan. Add the leeks to the pan and gently sweat, stirring

10–20 minutes

constantly. Separate 2 of the eggs and reserve the yolks. Lightly beat 3 whole eggs with 2 egg yolks, add the milk and season with salt and pepper.

20–30 minutes Remove the pastry from the oven and lift out the baking paper and baking beans. Line the bottom of the pastry with the pancetta and the leeks. Sprinkle over the grated cheese, then pour over the egg mixture and return to the oven for about 30 minutes, until set and golden brown on top.

30–40 minutes Whip the cream until stiff peaks form. Divide the cream in half and mix half with the lemon curd. Taste and add some icing sugar, depending upon the degree of tartness you like.

40–50 minutes Mix the remaining cream with the raspberries and some sugar, to taste. Fill 6 shot glasses with the lemon mixture and 6 with the raspberry mixture. Transfer to the fridge until ready to serve.

Tear the lettuce. Mix all the dressing ingredients together in a jar.

To serve Let the quiche cool a little before serving.

Dress and toss the salad and serve with the quiche.

Dress the top of the lemon pots with some grated dark chocolate and decorate the raspberry pots with some grated white chocolate. Serve each person a raspberry and a lemon pot on the same plate with a small spoon.

...and to drink *White Mâcon Villages*

Comfort Night In

€–€€

My mother-in-law introduced me to the tasty and fabulous main course dish. It's a firm favourite in our house.

Chicory wrapped in ham and baked in white sauce

Crisp green salad

Apple tartlets with vanilla ice cream

12 heads chicory	2 heads round lettuce	2 Granny Smith apples
75g butter		25g butter, melted
75g plain flour	**Dressing**	425g ready-rolled puff
1 litre milk	6 tbsp olive oil	pastry (2 sheets)
50g medium Cheddar	2 tbsp cider vinegar	4 tbsp sugar
cheese, grated	(homemade, if you	2 tsp cinnamon
12 slices cooked ham	can get it)	vanilla ice cream, to serve
salt and pepper	1 tsp Dijon mustard	
	salt and pepper	

0–10 minutes

Remove the outer layer of the chicory. Rinse the chicory in cold water. Using a sharp knife make a cross about 1cm deep in the base of each stem. Steam the chicory for about 12 minutes.

Core and cut the apples into little slices.

Melt the butter in a small heavy-based saucepan.

10–20 minutes

Add the flour to the butter and, using a hand-held balloon whisk, mix well. Allow the flour to be absorbed by the butter; you should have a thick paste. Add a little milk, stirring constantly with the whisk to get rid of any lumps. As the sauce begins to thicken add more milk until all the milk has been used. Season with salt and pepper. Cook

the sauce, stirring constantly with the whisk, until it has a rich smooth consistency. Be patient with it!

20–30 minutes

Remove the sauce from the heat and stir in 30g grated cheese. This will thicken the sauce a little more.

Remove the chicory heads from the steamer. Leave them to cool a little.

30–40 minutes

Roll out the pastry sheets and cut into squares. Line a baking tray with baking paper and place the squares on the tray. Brush each square with a little melted butter. Place some apple slices on each pastry square and brush with a little more butter. In a separate dish mix the sugar and cinnamon together. Sprinkle about a teaspoon of sugar and cinnamon over each tart.

40–50 minutes

Preheat the oven to 190°C/375F°/Gas Mark 5.

Wrap each chicory head in a slice of ham and place in an ovenproof dish. Don't line them up them too tightly as you want the sauce to coat each head of chicory. Pour the sauce over the chicory. Scatter the remaining grated cheese on top.

Put the chicory in the oven and bake for about 15 minutes until the cheese has melted, is bubbling slightly, and is just turning brown at the edges.

50–60 minutes

Tear the lettuce leaves into bite-sized pieces and place in a salad bowl. In a separate dish, mix all the dressing ingredients together.

To serve

Place the chicory on the table in its baking dish and allow your guests to serve themselves.

The salad can be served either with the chicory or afterwards. Dress and toss the salad just before serving.

About 15 minutes before dessert is to be served, place the apple tartlets in the preheated oven. Serve straight from the oven with vanilla ice cream.

...and to drink

Sancerre

His and Hers Movie Night In

Having spent many nights throwing together some pasta dishes this is by far my
favourite. I love the rich thick creamy sauce combined with the salty crisp fat of streaky
bacon. The salad is really an afterthought so that I don't feel guilty. As the topping of
the salad is more like a salsa I sometimes serve crisps with this starter. The pecan nuts
add an extra crunch and sweetness to the crumble. Served with whipped cream, this is
a truly indulgent finish to an indulgent meal.

€

Avocado salad

Spaghetti alla carbonara

Apple and plum pecan crumble with cream

8 vine-ripened tomatoes	16 rashers streaky bacon	200ml water
1 garlic clove	4 tbsp olive oil	2 large tbsp light brown sugar
2 small red onions	1kg dried spaghetti	6 large Bramley apples
1 handful chopped basil	4 eggs	6 plums
1 handful chopped parsley	6 tbsp single cream	1 tsp ground cinnamon
4 tbsp olive oil	100g Parmesan cheese, grated,	whipped cream, to serve
1 tsp sugar	plus extra for serving	
1 handful pine kernels	salt and freshly cracked	**Crumble topping**
4 ripe avocados	black pepper	200g plain flour
salt and pepper	chopped parsley, to garnish	120g caster sugar
Parmesan cheese		175g unsalted butter, chilled
shavings, to garnish		100g chopped pecan nuts
		1 tsp cinnamon

Heat the water with the sugar in a heavy-based saucepan. Peel, core and slice the
apples. Quarter and stone the plums. Place the apples in the saucepan with the water
and sugar, then add the cinnamon and cook for about 5 minutes. When the apples start

0–10 minutes

to soften remove the saucepan from the heat. Add the plums, cover the saucepan with a lid and allow the plums to stew in the apple juices.

10–20 minutes   Preheat the oven to 180°C/350°F/Gas Mark 4.

For the crumble topping: Mix the flour, sugar and a salt in a bowl. Cut the butter into small chunks and add this to the dry ingredients. Rub in, using the tips of your fingers, until the mixture resembles breadcrumbs.

Whiz the pecan nuts in the food processor, add to the flour and butter mixture, then add the cinnamon. Grease a baking dish with butter. Place the slightly stewed fruit at the bottom of the dish. Scatter the crumble thickly over the surface of the fruit. Resist pressing it down. Bake for 35–40 minutes until golden brown, with the juices bubbling up around the edges.

20–30 minutes

Chop the tomatoes into small chunks. Finely chop the garlic and onions and mix with the tomatoes, basil and parsley in a bowl. Add the oil and season with salt and pepper. Add the sugar and pine kernels and mix well. Cover with clingfilm and set aside for about 30 minutes to allow all the flavours to combine.

30–40 minutes

Chop the bacon rashers into small pieces. Heat 2 tablespoons of the oil in a large heavy-based saucepan, add the bacon and sauté until golden brown. Add the remaining oil to a large saucepan of lightly salted water and put it on to boil.

40–50 minutes

Thinly slice the avocados and arrange decoratively on a plate. Spread the tomato sauce over the sliced avocado. Season with salt and pepper and garnish with Parmesan cheese shavings.

50–60 minutes

Remove the crumble from the oven.

Place the salad in the centre of the table and allow your guests to serve themselves.

To serve

When the water reaches boiling point, add the spaghetti to the saucepan and continue boiling until it is *al dente*. Drain, add to the saucepan with the bacon and gently stir in the beaten eggs and cream. Season with salt and pepper. Stir over a low heat until the egg starts to set. Toss the spaghetti with the grated Parmesan cheese. Sprinkle with the chopped parsley. Set a little bowl of grated Parmesan cheese on the table along with some freshly cracked black pepper. (I usually bash a couple of peppercorns in a mortar to have good coarse pepper.)

Set your oven to low and heat through the crumble. Serve warm with whipped cream.

Orvieto or Frascati   **...and to drink**

Midweek recovery meal

This is my dear friend Catherine Walsh's recipe. What I loved about the dish was the lack of frills. No bouquet garni, no bay leaves, no thickeners – just plain basic ingredients. I don't know if she did it intentionally or had very little in her storecupboard. But whatever it was, it really hit the spot. The stew is best served in large flat bowls or pasta dishes.

€–€€

Black pudding salad with tomato relish and soldiers

Lamb stew

Irish whiskey bread and butter pudding

	Dressing	6 gigot lamb chops	1 brioche loaf
1 round of black pudding	3 tbsp olive oil	2 large onions	3 eggs
10 cherry tomatoes	1 tbsp red wine vinegar	4 carrots	150g sugar
1 small red onion	1 tsp maple syrup	3 celery sticks	300ml double cream
1 bag mixed salad leaves	2 tsp Dijon mustard	1 chicken stock cube	300ml milk
6 slices of toast		5 large potatoes	100ml Irish whiskey
butter		salt and pepper	½ tsp cinnamon
tomato relish, to serve		fresh flat-leaf parsley, to garnish	250g raisins
			icing sugar, for dusting

Brown the lamb in a heavy-based casserole dish (no need for any oil). Roughly chop the onions, add to the lamb and mix. Chop the carrots and the celery and add to the dish.

0–10 minutes

Break a stock cube into the stew, add enough water to cover all the ingredients and season with salt and pepper. Peel the potatoes and slice thickly. Layer the potatoes on top of the other ingredients. Cover the casserole dish and cook. The stew should cook for at least 1 hour.

10–20 minutes

20–30 minutes	Grease a baking dish with a little butter. Cut the brioche into thick slices. Cut the slices in half and arrange them in the baking dish. Whisk the eggs, sugar, cream, milk, whiskey and cinnamon together.
30–40 minutes	Pour the egg mixture over the bread and leave to soak for about 20 minutes. Add the raisins.
	Cut the black pudding into small rounds and fry in a frying pan or cook under a grill until crisp on both sides and soft in the centre. This will take about 8 minutes under the grill.
40–50 minutes	Preheat the oven to 190°C/375°F/Gas Mark 5.
	Cut the tomatoes in half. Finely slice the onion.
50–60 minutes	Put the bread pudding in the oven and bake for about 35 minutes.
	Mix all the dressing ingredients together in a large bowl. Add the salad leaves, tomatoes and onion and toss.
	Butter the toast and cut each slice into 3 thin strips.
To serve	Serve each person a portion of salad topped with about 2–3 small slices of black pudding, accompanied by the toast strips and with the tomato relish in a little dish on the side.
	Serve each person a large bowl of stew garnished with a sprig of parsley.
	The pudding is best served warm from the oven with cream. Before serving sift a little icing sugar over the top.
...and to drink	*South African Merlot/Cabernet Sauvignon* *Languedoc Syrah*

Mother's Day Lunch

The pea and mint soup is one of my staples. Even when someone pops in for lunch it takes only 10 minutes to throw it together and the results are fantastic. It will also make a great light supper served with a poached egg. If you find the vanilla froth a bit cheffy, there's no need to bother with it. It was once served to me in a restaurant like this so I thought it was fancy enough to be a treat for my mum. Assembling your own sponge gives the cake a homemade feel. You can always pretend you baked it yourself!

€€–€€€

Pea and mint soup with a vanilla froth

Herb-crusted cod with boiled potatoes and Joan's sauce

Lemon curd sponge cake

2 onions
3 shallots
3 tbsp olive oil
sprig of thyme
2 bay leaves
1 organic vegetable stock cube
450g petits pois
1 garlic clove
4–6 fresh mint leaves,
    plus extra to garnish
salt and pepper

Vanilla froth
1 vanilla pod
200ml milk

1kg baby potatoes
6 tbsp breadcrumbs
2 garlic cloves, crushed
6 tbsp chopped mixed herbs
    (parsley, dill and chives)
4 tbsp olive oil
2 tsp lemon juice
6 cod fillets, about 165g
    each (skin removed)
salt and pepper
slices of lemon, to garnish

Joan's sauce
50–100ml single cream
2 large tbsp mayonnaise
200g crème fraîche
2–3 drops Worcestershire
    sauce
2–3 drops tomato ketchup
¼ tsp mild curry powder
a squeeze of lemon juice
salt and pepper

1 x 20-cm round sponge
200ml double cream
lemon curd or jam of
    your choice
toasted flaked almonds,
    to decorate

Roughly chop the onions and shallots. Heat the oil in a large heavy-based saucepan and sweat the onions and shallots with the thyme and bay leaves. Dissolve the stock cube in 1 litre of boiling water.	**0–10 minutes**
Add about 750ml stock to the onions and shallots. Add the petits pois, bring to a simmer and cook for about 2 minutes. Remove the thyme and bay leaves. Whiz the soup in a blender and add the garlic and mint. Season to taste with salt and pepper. Add more stock to thin the soup if you find the consistency too thick.	**10–20 minutes**
For the sauce: Combine the mayonnaise and the crème fraîche in a bowl. Thin the mixture by adding some cream and a little lemon juice. Mix in the rest of the ingredients. Add more cream or lemon juice to taste. Set aside to chill in the fridge until you are ready to serve.	**20–30 minutes**
Bring a saucepan of lightly salted water to the boil. Put the potatoes in a steamer and place over the saucepan of boiling water.	**30–40 minutes**

Mix the breadcrumbs with the garlic and herbs. Mix the oil and lemon juice together on a plate.

40–50 minutes   Preheat the oven to 200°C/400°F/Gas Mark 6.

Lightly coat each side of the cod fillets with the oil and lemon juice. Season with a little salt and pepper and then coat the fish with the breadcrumb mixture. Place the fish on a baking tray.

For the froth: Cut the vanilla pod in half and place in a small saucepan with the milk. Heat the milk until it starts to simmer, remove from the heat and froth it. I do this by placing the milk in a cafetière or plunger pot and plunge it up and down to foam the milk.

Place the fish in the oven and bake for about 15 minutes.

Remove the potatoes from the steamer and toss in a little butter and the remaining herbs. The potatoes can be kept warm in the saucepan.

Gently reheat the soup.

To serve   Pour the soup into warmed bowls, top with a little dollop of froth and garnish with mint leaves. Serve with the brown bread and butter.

Serve the fish straight from the oven. Garnish each plate with a dollop of sauce and a slice of lemon. Place the potatoes in a decorative bowl in the centre of the table.

Cut the sponge cake in half horizontally and sandwich the halves together with some lemon curd. Whip the cream until it forms stiff peaks. Place the cream on top of the sponge and decorate with toasted flaked almonds. Serve with a fresh pot of tea made from loose tea, and mother will be in her element.

...and to drink   *Chablis*

Garden Party

My mother-in-law Françoise is a terrific cook and this is her signature pâté. It's ideal for serving on crisp rustic bread or even as a dip. Meringues are food science at its best. Although there are only two ingredients it's the method of combining and cooking them that makes the dish work. Follow the instructions exactly and you will have a perfect result.

€–€€

Françoise's mackerel pâté on rye toast

Fresh herb pasta

Homemade meringue with strawberries and cream

2 fillets smoked mackerel	2 garlic cloves	(makes about 20 small meringues)
1 small garlic clove	150g chopped fresh herbs	
200–250g thick natural yoghurt	125g pine kernels	3 large egg whites
1 lemon	135ml extra virgin olive oil	170g white caster sugar
salt and freshly cracked black pepper	(reserve 1 tbsp for the pasta cooking water)	400g organic strawberries
rye bread, to serve	750g dried farfalle pasta	250ml single cream
	125g Parmesan cheese, freshly grated	1 tbsp vanilla sugar
	sea salt and pepper	

Preheat the oven to 130°C/250°F/Gas Mark 1.

0–10 minutes

Put the egg whites into a large mixing bowl. Using an electric whisk, whisk them until they are stiff and peaked like snow-capped mountain tops. Add the sugar, about a teaspoon at a time, and keep whisking. A secret to good meringues is to make sure the sugar is thoroughly mixed in. You will notice while mixing in the sugar that the mixture

becomes shiny and stiff. When the mixture becomes almost impossible to whisk it's ready to go on a baking tray.

Cover a baking tray with baking paper. Use two tablespoons to scoop the mixture onto the tray, one spoon to scoop and the other to help you scrape the mixture off the first spoon. Leave a little room between each meringue as they expand when they cook. Put them in the oven. After an hour turn off the oven but leave the meringues to cool down in the oven. This will dry them out and make them crunchy.

10–20 minutes

Break the fish into little pieces and put them into a food processor. Make sure to take out all the bones. Add the garlic. Whiz the fish and the garlic until minced. Add the yoghurt and whiz again. It's best to add a little at a time so that you can control the texture of the spread – you don't want it too runny. Add a little lemon juice to lift the flavours.

20–30 minutes

Season with salt and lots of cracked black pepper. (Taste before seasoning – you may not need any salt as the fish can be rather salty.) Put the spread in a dish, cover with clingfilm and put in the fridge for about 30 minutes.

30–40 minutes

Cut the garlic cloves in half and remove the green stem from the middle. Put the herbs and garlic into a food processor and whiz until finely chopped.

40–50 minutes

Slice the rye bread and toast until crisp.

Dry-fry the pine kernels in a frying pan until they are golden brown.

Hull and quarter the strawberries and set them aside to reach room temperature.

Whip the cream and add the vanilla sugar.

Bring a large saucepan of lightly salted water to the boil with 1 tablespoon of oil.

Arrange the toast in a small basket.

To serve

Place the dish with the mackerel pâté in the centre of the table and allow your guests to help themselves.

By now the meringues should have been in the oven for an hour. Turn off the oven but leave the meringues in the oven.

Add the pasta to the saucepan of boiling water and cook until it is *al dente*. Drain the pasta and return to the saucepan, then add the herbs and the remaining oil. Mix well and season to taste with salt and pepper. Scatter the pine kernels on top and serve immediately with the grated Parmesan cheese on the side.

Remove the cooled meringues from the oven. Sandwich them together in pairs with some whipped cream and place on a serving plate. Scatter a few strawberries on the plate and dust with a little icing sugar.

...and to drink

White Rioja

Summer

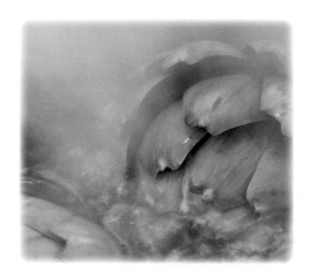

Al Fresco Dining

€€€ This meal really kick-starts the summer. It has all the elements that suggest warm nights and sunshine. It was my brother who introduced me to cooking duck in this way and my brother-in-law Etienne made this easy dip. The simple tarts came from a French student. Made with Wexford strawberries they not only look impressive but taste 'deeleeshus' (in a French accent).

Crisp summer vegetables with anchovy dip

Caramelised duck brochettes with rosemary and lemon potato wedges

Raspberry and strawberry tartlets

1 green pepper	1 tbsp runny honey	250ml milk
1 red pepper	2 tbsp soy sauce	2 eggs
1 yellow pepper	4 sprigs fresh rosemary	80g caster sugar
2 small fennel bulbs	3 duck breasts, about	30g plain flour
1kg cherry tomatoes	275–300g each	350g strawberries
	1kg potatoes	100g raspberries
Anchovy dip	3 tbsp olive oil	6 readymade tartlet cases
100g canned anchovy fillets	1 lemon	icing sugar, for dusting
2 garlic cloves	6 sprigs fresh rosemary	sprigs of fresh mint,
250ml olive oil	6 cloves garlic	to decorate
2 tsp lemon juice	salt and pepper	

0–10 minutes   Put some wooden skewers to soak in cold water.

In a large bowl combine the honey, soy sauce and rosemary. Cut each duck breast into thick strips – about 6 strips per breast. Mix the duck breast pieces with the honey, soy sauce and rosemary. Season with salt and pepper and set aside.

Heat the milk in a small saucepan. Separate the eggs. Using a hand-held balloon whisk beat the egg yolks and sugar together until they are pale in colour. Add the flour and mix well. Continue whisking the egg and sugar mixture while adding the warm milk very slowly. It's important to keep whisking so the milk does not cook the eggs. When all the milk has been added return the mixture to the saucepan and continue to whisk over a low heat until the cream no longer sticks to the sides. Remove from the heat and chill.

10–20 minutes

If using a charcoal barbecue it's best to light it now.

20–30 minutes

Peel the potatoes, cut them into chunky wedges, place all the wedges in a large baking dish and toss with the oil. Cut the lemon into chunks and scatter these among the potatoes. Scatter the whole cloves of garlic over the potatoes and tuck a couple of rosemary sprigs underneath.

Preheat the oven to 200°C/400°F/ Gas Mark 6.

30–40 minutes Cut the peppers into strips. Thinly slice the fennel. Cut the cherry tomatoes in half. Arrange all the raw vegetables on a platter.

Put the potatoes in the oven to cook. Toss them every now and then so they brown on all sides. This should take about 25–30 minutes.

40–50 minutes Thread 3 pieces of duck breast onto each skewer. Set aside.

For the dip: Using a food processor whiz the anchovies and garlic together.

50–60 minutes Put the anchovy paste in a heatproof bowl set over a saucepan of simmering water. Add the lemon juice and mix well using a hand-held balloon whisk. Add the oil a little at a time, whisking until all the oil has been incorporated and the dip has a thick consistency, almost like a mayonnaise.

To serve Serve the dip a little tepid with the vegetables on the side.

Cook the duck, skin side down, on the preheated barbecue, uncovered, until browned. Turn and cook for a further 1–2 minutes, depending upon how your guests like their duck. I usually turn the skewers when the skin is crisp and caramelised, then drizzle over the remaining juices and cook for a further minute. The duck tastes great when it is pink. Serve the potatoes straight from the oven.

Hull and quarter the strawberries. Mix the raspberries with the chilled cream. Spoon the raspberry cream mixture into the bottom of the tartlet cases and then arrange the strawberries decoratively on top. Dust with a little icing sugar and decorate with sprigs of fresh mint.

...and to drink *Pinot Noir Rosé*

Special Occasion Buffet

Whether you are serving a small or large gathering this menu is suitable. This is what I served to 50 guests for Míla's christening. I cheated a bit and bought the poppadoms from our local Indian takeaway.

€–€€

Oven-baked Kashmir chicken with coconut rice and poppadoms

Green salad

Vanilla ice cream with a mango coulis

2 onions, roughly chopped	400g long-grain rice	**Dressing**
2 garlic cloves	1 bay leaf	4 tbsp olive oil
2.5-cm piece root ginger	2 tbsp single cream	2 tbsp rapeseed oil
400ml natural yoghurt	finely chopped fresh	2 tbsp red wine vinegar
1 heaped tsp ground turmeric	coriander, to garnish	1 tsp runny honey
1 heaped tsp ground cumin	mango chutney and plain	salt and pepper
1 heaped tsp ground coriander	poppadoms, to serve	
1 tsp hot chilli powder		**3 mangoes**
6 x 100g boneless, skinless	2 heads lettuce	**2–3 tbsp lemon juice**
chicken breasts	3 scallions (spring onions)	**icing sugar, to taste**
50g ground almonds		**1 tub good quality**
100g creamed coconut		**vanilla ice cream**

Whiz the onions in a food processor. Heat some oil in a frying pan, add the onions and gently sauté for about 2 minutes. Clean the food processor and whiz the garlic, ginger and yoghurt together.

0–10 minutes

Preheat the oven to 190°C/375°F/Gas Mark 5.

10–20 minutes

When you start to smell the onion cooking, add all the spices. Stir quickly, then remove from the heat to allow the flavours of the spices to be released. Cut each chicken breast into 6 pieces. Mix the onions with the yoghurt mixture and add the almonds. Arrange the chicken in a casserole dish and pour over the sauce.

20–30 minutes   Cover the chicken with foil, put it in the oven and cook for about 15 minutes.

Peel the mango, remove the stone and cut the fruit into bite-sized chunks. Whiz the mango with the lemon juice in a liquidiser or food processor until smooth. Add icing

sugar to taste. The amount of sugar you use depends on the ripeness of the mangoes. Add a teaspoon at a time.

Bring 800ml water to the boil in a large saucepan.   **30–40 minutes**

Tear the lettuce leaves. Finely chop the scallion.

Roughly chop the creamed coconut. Add the creamed coconut to the boiling water and stir until it is dissolved. Add the rice and bay leaf, bring back to the boil, cover and simmer for 15 minutes, stirring occasionally until the rice is tender and the liquid has been absorbed.

Remove the foil from the chicken and cook for a further 15 minutes.

Mix all the ingredients for the salad dressing in a jar.   **40–50 minutes**

Cook the poppadoms one at a time in a microwave oven for about 25–30 seconds each on Medium.

Check the rice – If it is tender remove it from the heat.   **50–60 minutes**

Remove the chicken from the oven, add the cream and stir. Cover with the foil and set aside until you are ready to serve.

Put the poppadoms in a basket on the table. Put the rice in a serving dish. Just before   **To serve**
putting the chicken on the table, garnish it with some chopped coriander and serve with the dish of rice. Serve the mango chutney on the side.

Toss the salad with the dressing just before serving. Serve with or after the chicken dish.

Serve each person a portion of ice cream drizzled with the mango coulis.

Riesling   **...and to drink**
Beer

Classic American Barbecue

€–€€

I spent many summers working at The Red Parrot bar and restaurant in Newport, Rhode Island. Salads and desserts were my speciality. It was here that I learned how to make the perfect Caesar salad. When made using a homemade dressing it's pure lush. The potato salad is my mother's signature dish – always a favourite for any barbecue. Mum always added a secret ingredient and when asked what it was she would say 'TLC'. I guess that's why it always tasted so good.

Caesar Salad

Hamburgers with American-style potato salad

Strawberries dipped in chocolate sauce

50g canned anchovy fillets

2 garlic cloves

2 egg yolks

1 tsp Tabasco sauce

1 tsp Worcestershire sauce

juice of ½ lemon

200ml sunflower oil

100ml olive oil

2 heads Romaine lettuce

50g Parmesan cheese shavings

Croûtons

6 small bread rolls

3–4 tbsp olive oil

pepper

1 garlic clove

2 shallots

1 egg

1kg round steak mince

2 tsp finely chopped thyme

salt and pepper

sunflower oil, for brushing

To serve

6–8 hamburger buns

1 tomato

American-style mustard

lettuce leaves

Potato salad

1kg new potatoes of
    similar size

3 eggs

2 celery sticks

handful fresh parsley

3 scallions (spring onions)

3–5 tbsp mayonnaise

1 tbsp American-style mustard

salt

800g strawberries

200g plain chocolate

30g cocoa powder

175g caster sugar

300ml milk

0–10 minutes	Crush the garlic. Finely chop the shallot. Lightly beat the egg. Mix the mince with the thyme, garlic, shallot, salt and pepper and just enough of the beaten egg to bind without making the mixture sloppy.
10–20 minutes	If using a charcoal barbecue, light the coals now.
	Divide the mixture into 8 (someone always wants another). Shape into round burgers about 2.5cm thick. Cover the burgers loosely with clingfilm and chill in the fridge.
	Preheat the oven to 200°C/400°F/Gas Mark 6.
20–30 minutes	*For the croûtons*: Cut the bread rolls into slices. Rub with the oil and toast in the oven for about 6–10 minutes until crisp and brown on both sides. Set aside to cool.
	For the potato salad: Bring a large saucepan of lightly salted water to the boil. Add the potatoes and simmer for about 10–15 minutes. Test with a fork – they should be soft but not mushy.
30–40 minutes	Drain the potatoes thoroughly and rinse under cold running water.

Bring a small saucepan of water to the boil. Lower the eggs into the water on a spoon, one at a time. Reduce the heat and simmer for 10 minutes.

Finely slice the celery. Finely chop the parsley and the scallions.

Rinse the eggs under cold running water.

40–50 minutes

In a food processor pulse the anchovy fillets, garlic, egg yolks, Tabasco sauce, Worcestershire sauce and lemon juice. Gradually add the oil and pulse as you go. When all the oil has been added thin the dressing by adding some water. Season to taste with pepper. You may wish to add more lemon juice.

Hull the strawberries.

For the potato salad: In a large salad bowl combine all the ingredients and season with salt and pepper. Finely slice the tomatoes and tear the lettuce leaves.

Brush the hamburgers with some oil on each side. Grill them for about 4–5 minutes on each side until nicely browned.

In a large bowl toss the lettuce with the croûtons in some of the dressing and top with Parmesan shavings. Serve immediately.

To serve

Lightly toast the buns. Serve the hamburgers hot on a bun with a slice of tomato, a dollop of mustard and a bit of lettuce.

Put the chocolate, cocoa powder, sugar and milk into a saucepan. Stir over a low heat until the chocolate and sugar have dissolved. Increase the heat until it starts to bubble, then reduce the heat and simmer for about 6 minutes. Place the saucepan on the rack of the barbecue over a low heat and allow your guests to dunk their strawberries.

Californian Chardonnay, to start
Zinfandel

...and to drink

Indoor Barbecue

€–€€

I adore corn on the cob. I have very fond childhood memories of chewing on ears of corn. My Grandma always cooked them in a little milk, which would tenderise them a little more. The couscous salad can be adapted to any meal – the colours and texture will always be terrific.

Corn on the cob

Marinated pork chops with a Mediterranean couscous salad

Fresh strawberries and cream with a French twist

300ml milk

1 tsp sugar

6 ears of corn (tender and
   fresh, if possible)

butter, pepper and coarse
   sea salt, to serve

juice of 1 large lemon

1 tbsp Italian seasoning

2 garlic cloves, crushed

6 tbsp extra virgin olive oil

6 large pork chops

pepper

Couscous salad

juice of 3 lemons

500g couscous

2 tbsp olive oil

1 cucumber

1 large Spanish onion

6 tomatoes

2 tbsp fresh mint

2 tbsp fresh flat-leaf parsley

handful stoned black olives

salt and pepper

400g fresh strawberries

1 tbsp lemon juice

caster sugar and whipped
   cream, to serve

0–10 minutes

Mix the lemon juice, Italian seasoning, garlic and oil together and season with a little pepper. Using a sharp knife snip the fat around the edge of the chops at 1-cm intervals. Coat the chops in the marinade. Cover with clingfilm and put in the fridge.

10–20 minutes	*For the couscous salad*: Bring a large saucepan of water to the boil. Remove from the heat and add the lemon juice. Put the couscous into a large heatproof bowl and pour over enough water so the couscous is covered, with about 2cm of water to spare. Cover the bowl with a plate and leave to stand for about 5 minutes until the grains swell.
20–30 minutes	Using a fork fluff the couscous and add the oil. Fluff again until cool. Peel the cucumber and finely chop. Finely chop the onion. Remove the pulp from the tomatoes and finely chop the flesh. Finely chop the mint and parsley. Roughly chop the olives.
30–40 minutes	Add the remaining ingredients to the couscous, season with salt and pepper and leave to stand for about 20 minutes so that all the flavours combine.
40–50 minutes	Quarter the strawberries and toss them in the lemon juice.
	Remove the husks and silky threads from the corn.
50–60 minutes	Add the milk and sugar to a large saucepan of water and bring to the boil. Add the corn and cook for about 8–10 minutes. Overcooking will make the corn tough so be careful with the timing. When cooked, drain and place in a dish covered with a clean tea towel.
	Preheat the grill to medium.
To serve	Serve the corn immediately with some butter, pepper and salt. If you don't have corn skewers supply your guests with napkins so they can grab hold of the ears.
	Place the grill rack under the grill so that the meat is about 10cm from the heat. Remove the chops from the marinade, place on the grill rack and cook. Depending upon the thickness of the chops allow 6–8 minutes on each side, until they are lightly browned and cooked right through. Serve immediately, with the couscous.
	Serve the strawberries with a small bowl of caster sugar and some whipped cream on the side. Allow your guests to sweeten the strawberries to their liking.
...and to drink	*New World Syrah* *Beer*

Moroccan nights

Food became a high priority during an extraordinary cycling adventure through the Atlas Mountains. At the end of every day François and I would light a fire and marinate whatever meat we had, usually goat, in our spices and cook it over the fire. I have very fond memories of the flavours – any meat marinated in our spices tasted fantastic. This meal can also be made for large parties.

€€–€€€

Crayfish salad

Moroccan lamb brochettes with pitta bread and cucumber dip

Fresh cherries

4 tbsp extra virgin olive oil

juice of 1 lemon

1 head Iceberg (Webbs) lettuce

large handful rocket

450g crayfish in brine

handful snipped chives

salt and pepper

1kg tenderloin of lamb

2 red onions

2 red peppers

1 tbsp chopped fresh coriander

1 tbsp chopped fresh parsley

pitta bread, to serve

Marinade

4 tbsp olive oil

2 garlic cloves, crushed

zest and juice of 1 lemon

½ tsp ground cumin

½ tsp cinnamon

½ tsp ground coriander

½ tsp cayenne pepper

1 tbsp chopped fresh coriander

1 tbsp chopped fresh parsley

salt and pepper

Cucumber dip

½ cucumber

250ml natural yoghurt

freshly cracked black pepper

Fresh cherries

If using wooden skewers, put them to soak them in cold water.

0–10 minutes

Cut the lamb into cubes.

Mix all the marinade ingredients together. Add the lamb and toss to coat. Leave to marinate for at least 40 minutes.

10–20 minutes

If using a charcoal barbecue. light the coals now.

20–30 minutes

Cut the onion into quarters. Cut the peppers into large cubes.

For the dip: Peel and finely chop the cucumber. Mix the cucumber and yoghurt together and season with pepper.

If using a gas or electric barbecue, preheat to medium–high.

30–40 minutes

Rinse the crayfish in fresh water and then toss in half the lemon juice.

Thread the lamb cubes and the onion and pepper pieces alternately onto skewers.

40–50 minutes

Combine the oil and the remaining lemon juice together in a bowl. Add the lettuce and rocket leaves and toss. Taste and season as required. Sprinkle the crayfish and chives on top.

50–60 minutes

Place the large bowl with the crayfish salad in the centre of the table and allow your guests to serve themselves.

To serve

Cook the meat on the barbecue for about 3 minutes on each side. Turn the skewers occasionally until the meat is cooked evenly and browned. Place the skewers on a platter and scatter over the coriander and parsley.

Heat the pitta breads by placing them on the barbecue for a couple of seconds.

Serve the cucumber dip with the lamb.

Serve the cherries in a large bowl with some small ramekins on the side for the stones.

Rosé, to start
Côtes du Rhône

...and to drink

Sizzling Summer

€€€–€€€€

I just adore strawberries in sweet rosé wine and I can't think of nicer strawberries to use than the delicious Wexford strawberries for sale at the side of the road. I never feel as if summer has arrived until I see the fruit stalls at the roadside.

Grilled prawns with mango and herb salsa

Teriyaki steak and stir-fried vegetables

Strawberries in sweet rosé wine

1 garlic clove	1 tbsp grated ginger	2 yellow peppers
2 tbsp chopped parsley	1 garlic clove	¼ head white cabbage
2 tbsp chopped basil	2 mangoes, peeled, stoned	110g tender stem broccoli,
juice of 1 lemon	and finely chopped	cut into strips
1 tbsp Dijon mustard	2 tbsp orange juice	3 carrots, cut into matchsticks
5 tbsp olive oil	1 tbsp sugar	3 tbsp sunflower oil
500g fresh prawns	salt and pepper	2 garlic cloves, finely chopped
salt and pepper		1 tbsp grated root ginger
	250ml bottled teriyaki marinade	2 tbsp soy sauce
Mango and herb salsa		
½ red chilli	6 fillet steaks, about	**800g strawberries**
1 tbsp olive oil	1.5 cm thick	**300ml rosé wine**
1 red onion, finely chopped	2 red peppers	**4 tbsp sugar**

0–10 minutes   Pour the teriyaki marinade over the steaks and set aside.

Crush the garlic and combine with the parsley, basil and lemon juice. Add the mustard and oil and season with salt and pepper.

10–20 minutes   Put some wooden skewers to soak in cold water.

If using a charcoal barbecue it's best to light it now.

Pour the marinade over the prawns and set aside for at least 40 minutes.

For the salsa: Deseed the chilli and finely chop the flesh.

20–30 minutes   Gently heat the oil and sauté the onion. Add the ginger and garlic. Add the mango, orange juice, sugar and chopped chilli. Mix well and cook for about 10 minutes over a low heat. Season to taste with salt and pepper.

30–40 minutes   Remove the salsa from the heat and set aside to cool.

Hull and quarter the strawberries. Gently heat the wine just enough to dissolve the sugar, add the sugar and set aside to cool when it has dissolved.

Deseed the peppers and cut into strips. Core and shred the cabbage.

Pour the wine and sugar mixture over the strawberries, mix, then return to the fridge.

Thread the prawns onto the skewers. Place them on the hot barbecue and cook for about 20 seconds each side.

To serve   Serve straight from the barbecue with the salsa on the side.

Place the steaks on the barbecue and cook for about 4–6 minutes each side.

Place a wok over a high heat and heat until it smokes. Add the oil and swirl around. Add the garlic and ginger and stir-fry until they colour. Add the carrots and broccoli and stir-fry for about 2 minutes. Add the peppers and cabbage and continue to stir-fry for about 4 minutes. Add the soy sauce. Toss and serve immediately.

Serve the strawberries without any accompaniments.

...and to drink   *Champagne, to start*
New World Cabernet Sauvignon Merlot

All' Italia

One of my favourite things about summer is eating artichokes. Boil them until tender, then eat them leaf by leaf, dipping them into the vinaigrette and scraping away the flesh with your teeth. We always debate whether you should open up the artichoke fully and pour the vinaigrette into the centre or just start from the outside and work your way in to the heart, dipping each leaf into the sauce on the side. It really doesn't matter, it's all a question of preference. The same goes for the starter. Choose a nice mixture of ingredients to make a summer antipasti platter.

€€–€€€

Olives, pickled anchovies, semi sun-dried tomatoes and roasted peppers

---

Whole artichokes with vinaigrette dressing

Apple filo tartlets

2 different types of olive	6 large whole artichokes	2 eating apples
pickled anchovies	1 lemon	1 tbsp raisins
semi sun-dried tomatoes	4 eggs	1 tbsp walnuts, broken
roasted peppers	salt	1 tbsp lemon juice
rustic bread, to serve		2 tbsp sugar
	Dressing	1 tsp cinnamon
	12 tbsp olive oil	25g butter
	4 tbsp red wine vinegar	readymade filo pastry sheets
	2 tbsp Dijon mustard	icing sugar, for dusting
	salt and pepper	crème fraîche, to serve

Trim the tough tops of the artichoke leaves and a little bit of the stems. Bring 2 large saucepans of lightly salted water to the boil and add the lemon juice. Add the artichokes and cook for about 45–60 minutes depending on their size.

0–10 minutes

Put the eggs in a small saucepan of water and bring to the boil. Boil for about 5 minutes.

10–20 minutes

Peel and core the apples and cut into small chunks.

Mix the apples with the raisins, walnuts, lemon juice, sugar and cinnamon. Melt the butter.

20–30 minutes

Cut the pastry sheets into squares. Brush the inside of each of 6 metal fondant moulds with butter, then brush each side of the pastry sheets with butter and line each mould with 3 sheets. Let the sheets dangle over the top as these will be folded in to close.

30–40 minutes

Preheat the oven to 180°C/350°F/Gas Mark 4.

40–50 minutes

Spoon a tablespoon of the apple mixture into each mould. Fold over the pastry and add a little more if required. Brush the tops with butter. Place all the moulds on a baking tray, put them in the oven and bake for about 20 minutes.

Mix all the ingredients for the dressing together in a bowl. Shell the eggs and cut them into small pieces. Add to the vinaigrette and mix well. Season well with salt and pepper.

50–60 minutes

Arrange all the ingredients for the starter on a serving platter. Slice the bread.

Place the serving platter on the table and allow your guests to help themselves.

To serve

Put the vinaigrette into a bowl and place on the table. Give each person an artichoke on a plate.

Remove the apple tartlets from the moulds, dust with a little icing sugar and serve each one with a dollop of crème fraîche.

Loire Valley Beaujolais

...and to drink

Vive la France!

€€€ Sardines don't have to be just for hot summers in France. If it rains, as it usually will in Ireland, they will cook perfectly under a grill or in a ridged griddle pan. They do leave a fishy smell when grilled, so I usually burn some scented oils when they're cooked. Sardines taste best cooked over hot charcoal, so make sure to light the barbecue well in advance.

Selection of olives, semi sun-dried tomatoes and roasted peppers

Grilled sardines with a salted caper and tomato salad

Tarte au citron

olives	**Salted caper and tomato salad**	butter, for greasing
semi sun-dried tomatoes		flour, for dusting
roasted peppers	2 heads lettuce, torn	225g ready-rolled
	400g cherry tomatoes, halved	shortcrust pastry
1.5kg fresh sardines	½ red onion, thinly sliced	2 eggs
(about 3 per person)	1 tbsp capers in brine	200g sugar
2 tbsp olive oil		2 lemons
freshly cracked black pepper	**Dressing**	100ml double cream
lemon wedges, to serve	3 tbsp olive oil	icing sugar, for dusting
	1 tbsp cider vinegar	
	1 tbsp Dijon mustard	**To serve**
	1 tbsp runny honey	100ml whipping cream
	salt and pepper	1 tbsp vanilla sugar
		100g fresh raspberries

0–10 minutes   If using a charcoal barbecue, light the coals now.

Preheat the oven to 170°C/325°F/Gas Mark 3.

Grease a 20-cm tart tin with a little butter and dust with flour. Line the tart tin with pastry. Trim the edges and prick the bottom a couple of times using a small fork. Line the pastry with baking paper, fill it with baking beans, place in the oven and bake for 10–12 minutes.

10–20 minutes Using an electric whisk beat the eggs and sugar together until they are pale in colour. Grate the zest of 1 lemon and squeeze the juice of 2. Gradually add the lemon zest and juice to the egg and sugar mixture. In a separate bowl whip the cream. Fold the cream into the egg, lemon and sugar mixture. Remove the pastry case from the oven.

20–30 minutes Remove the baking beans and paper and pour the filling into the pastry case. Return the tart to the oven and bake for about 30–35 minutes until it is slightly golden on top and no longer wobbles when jiggled.

30–40 minutes Using a small sharp pair of scissors cut open the bellies of the sardines and remove the innards. Rinse the insides out and dry with kitchen paper. Drizzle a little oil over the fish and rub it in until they are lightly coated all over.

40–50 minutes *For the salad*: Place the lettuce, tomatoes and onion in a salad bowl. Combine all the ingredients for the dressing in a jar and shake well.

50–60 minutes Add the salted capers to the salad.

The sardines will need very little time to cook – about 2 minutes on each side.

Remove the tart from the oven.

To serve Serve the olives, tomatoes and peppers with some wine.

Dress and toss the salad. Serve the sardines on a large platter in the centre of the table with the lemon wedges on the side. Season with pepper.

Sift a little icing sugar over the top of the tart. Whip the cream with the vanilla sugar. Serve each person a slice of tart with a dollop of cream and some raspberries.

...and to drink *Soave*

Thai Style

I adore the fragrance and flavours of this meal. My dear sister-in-law Siobhan regularly makes this for her dinner parties. Served on a chilly summer's evening it's an ideal dinner for even a large group of people. Do make sure to get some good quality prawns and fish, as these will make the dish.

€€€–€€€€

Prawn crackers with a cucumber relish

Thai prawn and fish curry with mangetout and mango

Mango sorbet

5 tbsp rice wine vinegar	1.2 litres coconut milk	500g raw king prawn tails
135g caster sugar	2 red chillies	500g cod fillet
1 small red chilli	zest and juice of 1 lime	500g haddock fillet
75g roasted peanuts	25g root ginger	450g Thai jasmine rice
½ cucumber	4 cloves garlic	1 mango
½ small red onion	2 lemon grass stalks	200g mangetout
1 tsp fish sauce	1 small onion	handful fresh coriander
prawn crackers, to serve	3 tbsp fish sauce	leaves, to garnish
	1 tbsp runny honey	
		1 tub mango sorbet

Put all the coconut milk into a large heavy-based casserole dish and bring to the boil. Reduce the heat and cook until the fat separates from the solids. This will take about 20 minutes – stir occasionally and ignore the curdled appearance.

0–10 minutes

Slice off the stem ends of the chillies and deseed. Whiz the lime zest and juice, ginger, garlic, chillies, lemon grass, onion, fish sauce and honey together in a food processor to make a paste.

10–20 minutes

Rinse the prawns under cold running water. Skin the fish and cut into 4-cm chunks. Peel the mango and cut into 2-cm cubes.

Add the Thai curry paste to the coconut milk, and stir.

Put the vinegar and sugar in a small saucepan with 125ml water and bring to the boil. Reduce the heat and simmer for 5 minutes. Deseed the chilli and cut into thin strips.

Whiz the peanuts in a food processor until roughly chopped. Peel and deseed the cucumber and cut the flesh into small cubes.

Finely chop the onion. Allow the sauce to cool slightly before adding the chilli, peanuts, cucumber, onion and fish sauce. Place the prawn crackers, a few at a time, in a microwave oven and heat for about 40 seconds on High. Should the crackers overcook or undercook adjust the timing. Bring a large saucepan of lightly salted water to the boil.

Add the rice to the boiling water and cook for about 12 minutes.

Bring the coconut milk back to the boil. Add the prawns, mangetout and mango and cook for about 6 minutes. Add the fish and cook for a further 5 minutes.

When cooked the prawn crackers will form little bowls. Spoon the cucumber relish into the prawn cracker cups and serve.

Serve each person a portion of rice and a portion of curry garnished with a few fresh coriander leaves. If you have enough small bowls it's nice to serve the rice in one with the fish curry on the side.

Remove the sorbet from the freezer and serve.

South African Sauvignon

20–30 minutes

30–40 minutes

40–50 minutes

50–60 minutes

To serve

...and to drink

Provençal Supper

€€–€€€

My father always cooked potatoes in this way. He's a great man for the one-pot wonders and instead of grilled hake he would mix in a tin of tuna. But, for a refined dinner party, go for the hake.

Grilled hake with a lemon-tarragon sauce and Mediterranean potatoes

Sweet lemon cheese and biscuits

olive oil, for brushing
6 hake fillets, about 175g each
pepper

Lemon-tarragon sauce
2 tbsp water
1 tbsp balsamic vinegar
3 tbsp extra virgin olive oil
1 garlic clove, crushed
2 small shallots, finely chopped
1 tbsp finely chopped tarragon
1 tbsp grated lemon rind
salt and pepper

Mediterranean potatoes
12 potatoes
1 onion, finely chopped
1 tbsp olive oil
2 garlic cloves, crushed
800g canned chopped
   tomatoes
1 tbsp sugar
25g semi sun-dried tomatoes
100g stoned black olives
30g Parmesan cheese shavings
salt and pepper

450g mascarpone cheese
rind and juice of 1 lemon
75–100g caster sugar
assorted sweet biscuits
   (brandy snaps, shortbread,
   ginger snaps), to serve

0–10 minutes

For the sauce: Mix together the water, vinegar, oil and garlic and add the shallots, tarragon and lemon rind. Mix well, season with salt and pepper and set aside to allow all the flavours to combine.

10–20 minutes

For the potatoes: Bring a saucepan of lightly salted water to the boil. Cut the potatoes into 5-cm slices. Place the potato slices in a steamer set over the saucepan of boiling water and steam for about 8–10 minutes until tender but not breaking up.

20–30 minutes	Fry the onion in 1 tablespoon of the oil for about 3 minutes. Add the garlic, canned tomatoes and sugar. Stir and simmer for about 10–15 minutes.
	Remove the potatoes from the heat.
30–40 minutes	Chop the sun-dried tomatoes and add to the tomato sauce with two thirds of the olives. Season with salt and pepper. When the sauce has thickened mix it with the potatoes and put the mixture in a baking dish. Top with the remaining olives and Parmesan cheese shavings.
	Preheat the grill to medium.
40–50 minutes	Brown the potatoes under the grill.
	Using an electric beater cream the mascarpone cheese with the lemon rind and juice. With the beater still going add sugar to taste, transfer to the fridge and chill.
50–60 minutes	Line a baking tray with foil. Lightly brush the fish with oil on both sides and arrange them, skin side up, in a single layer on the baking tray. Season with pepper.
	The potatoes can be kept warm in the oven while the fish is cooking.
	Place the hake fillets under the grill so they are about 10cm from the heat. Grill them for about 6–8 minutes, depending upon the thickness of the fillets. After about 8 minutes remove the fish from the grill, cover with a dish and leave them to cook in their own heat for about 2 minutes.
To serve	Place the fillets, with their juices, on a warmed serving dish and spoon over the sauce. Serve the potatoes hot from the oven.
	Serve the lemon cheese with an assortment of sweet biscuits and a glass of dessert wine.
...and to drink	*Sauvignon Blanc or Tursan* *Muscat, to finish*

Grilled to Impress

My mother's Victoria plum tree produced an amazing yield of fruit a number of years ago and since then we have been poaching plums. This is a great dessert to make when the fruits are not so ripe.

€€–€€€

Crab salad

Penne de Côte d'Azur

Plum compôte

400g crabmeat	2 aubergines	4 tbsp chopped fresh parsley
2 tbsp snipped chives,	2 courgettes	50g Parmesan cheese, grated
plus extra to garnish	1 large red onion	salt and pepper
2 tbsp chopped parsley	4 field mushrooms	
zest and juice of 1 lemon	1 red pepper	500g plums
2 drops Tabasco sauce	3–4 tbsp olive oil	250ml water
salt 1 head Iceberg (Webbs)	1 stalk fresh thyme	250g caster sugar
lettuce, to serve	3 tbsp balsamic vinegar	1 tbsp lemon juice
	500g dried penne pasta	natural yoghurt, to serve
	zest of 1 lemon	sprigs of fresh mint, to decorate

Halve the plums.

0–10 minutes

Make a sugar syrup by bringing the water to the boil in a saucepan and dissolving the sugar in it. Add the lemon juice.

When the syrup is bubbling a little add the plums. Reduce the heat, stir, cover the saucepan and simmer for about 15 minutes.

10–20 minutes

If using a charcoal barbecue, light the coals now.

Cut the aubergines and courgettes into 1-cm strips. Slice the onion into thick rounds. Wipe the mushrooms clean. Deseed the pepper and slice into thick strips.

Remove the plums from the heat. Transfer to a bowl and set aside to cool.   **20–30 minutes**

Brush all the vegetables with some oil.

Mix the crabmeat with the chives and parsley. Add salt to taste. Cover with clingfilm and   **30–40 minutes**
place in the fridge.

Cook the vegetables directly over the hot coals, turning once, until nicely browned. This   **40–50 minutes**
should take about 5–7 minutes per side.

Bring a large saucepan of lightly salted water to the boil.

Remove the thyme leaves from the stalk and chop them a little.

Slice the cooked vegetables. While still warm place in a bowl and toss with the vinegar.   **50–60 minutes**

Add the pasta to the saucepan of boiling water.

Remove the crab from the fridge and add the lemon juice and Tabasco sauce. Put a   **To serve**
small bed of lettuce on each plate, top with some crab and garnish with snipped chives.

Drain the pasta when it is *al dente*. Place the pasta in a serving bowl, add the oil and
toss. Add the vegetables and their juices. Add the lemon zest, parsley, thyme and salt
and pepper. Sprinkle the cheese over the top and serve immediately.

Serve the plums straight from the fridge with a tablespoon of yoghurt per serving,
decorated with sprigs of fresh mint.

Sauvignon Blanc, to start
Barbaresco   **...and to drink**

Going Veggie

€ A good American friend of mine introduced me to aubergines cooked in this way. Of course she called it chicken-fried eggplant. As a child I did once ask which part of the chicken was used to make chicken-fried eggplant. Unfortunately, at the time, we were in a small diner in the back end of Texas and the restaurant went silent while Papa explained that the method of frying is the same method used to fry chicken. The same applies to steak. I was only 11, after all.

Melanzane fritte con Parmigiano

Pappardelle pomodoro, served with a green salad

Fresh peaches

2 aubergines	2 onions	fresh basil	**Dressing**
6 slices stale bread	4 garlic cloves	salt and pepper	3 tbsp olive oil
3 garlic cloves	2 tbsp olive oil	Parmesan cheese	1 tbsp white wine
25g Parmesan	400g canned tomatoes	shavings and	vinegar
cheese, grated	680g passata	sprigs of fresh	1 tsp maple syrup
8 tbsp sunflower oil	375g sweet red	basil, to garnish	1 tsp Dijon mustard
4 tbsp seasoned flour	pepper sauce		salt and pepper
2 eggs, beaten	2 tsp dried oregano	**Green salad**	
1 lemon	2 tbsp sugar	2 heads lettuce	**6 fresh peaches**
salt and pepper	500g fresh pappardelle	1 small red onion	
sprigs of fresh parsley	pasta		
to garnish	1 tbsp chopped		

0–10 minutes   Place the onions and 3 garlic cloves in a food processor and whiz until chopped. Heat about 2 tablespoons of the oil in a saucepan, add the onions and garlic and sweat.

10–20 minutes   Add the tomatoes, passata and sweet pepper sauce to the saucepan. Stir and add the

oregano and sugar. Season with salt and pepper and simmer over a low heat for about 20 minutes.

20–30 minutes   Slice each aubergine lengthways into about 6 slices. Sprinkle with salt and set aside for about 20 minutes.

30–40 minutes   Whiz the bread in a food processor to make really fine breadcrumbs. Finely chop the garlic. Mix the breadcrumbs, garlic and cheese together.

40–50 minutes   Remove the sauce from the heat and grate in the remaining garlic clove. Stir and set aside.

Heat the oil in a large frying pan. Take 3 large dishes – put the seasoned flour in one, the beaten egg in the second and the breadcrumb mixture in the third. Dip the aubergine slices first in the flour, then in the egg and then in the breadcrumbs, to coat. Fry the slices until golden brown. This will take seconds.

Preheat the oven to 80°C/175°F/Gas Mark ¼.

Transfer the fried aubergine slices to a plate lined with kitchen paper and put them in the oven.

Put a large saucepan of lightly salted water on to boil.

For the salad: Finely slice the red onion.

To serve   When all the aubergine slices are cooked drizzle with a little lemon juice, garnish with some fresh parsley and serve.

Mix all the dressing ingredients together in a salad bowl. Add the lettuce and onion and toss.

Add the pasta to the boiling water and cook for 3–4 minutes. Drain the pasta and toss with some of the sauce. Season with pepper. Add some chopped basil and sprinkle with Parmesan cheese shavings and sprigs of fresh basil. Serve with the salad.

Serve the peaches whole, without any accompaniments.

...and to drink   *Dolcetto*

Autumn

Warm Weekend Evening

€–€€

This is François' favourite dinner. He just adores grilled mackerel fillets. My parents-in-law have a massive fig tree growing in their garden. Luckily each year it produces the most delicious fruit. If the figs are ripe there is no need for fancy recipes – simply serve them as a starter with Parma ham or on their own for dessert.

Figs with Parma ham

Grilled mackerel fillets with a lemon caper butter dressing, roast potatoes wedges with lemon and thyme, roast cherry tomatoes and baby spinach

---

Pineapple caramelised in white rum

6 very ripe figs	4 garlic cloves	2 tsp caster sugar
12–18 very thin slices Parma ham	500g cherry tomatoes on the vine	500g fresh baby leaf spinach
fresh rocket, to garnish	50g butter	coarse sea salt
	juice of ½ lemon	pepper
6 large potatoes	3 tbsp capers, drained	**1 large pineapple**
5 tbsp olive oil	1 tbsp whole-grain Dijon mustard	**3 tbsp white rum**
½ lemon, cut into bite-sized chunks	6–12 fresh mackerel fillets, depending on size	**2 tbsp caster sugar**
4 sprigs thyme		**thick Greek-style yoghurt, to serve**

0–10 minutes

Preheat the oven to 220°C/425°F/Gas Mark 7.

Cut each potato into quarters then cut each quarter lengthways into 2 or 3 long wedges.

10–20 minutes

Put 3 tablespoons of the oil into a large shallow baking tray. Put the tray in the oven for about 2 minutes to heat the oil. Remove the tray from the oven and carefully place

the potatoes wedges, lemon chunks, thyme and garlic in a single layer in the hot tray. Season with coarse sea salt and toss the wedges in the oil using a spoon. Place in the oven and bake for about 35 minutes, turning every 15 minutes or so until they are browned on the outside and soft in the centre.

Cut the pineapple into bite-sized chunks. Put the pineapple chunks into a large casserole dish with the rum and sugar. Cook over a low heat until the pineapple starts to soften. Remove from the heat and set aside to cool slightly.

20–30 minutes

30–40 minutes	Take the potatoes out of the oven, toss and return to the oven.
	Cut the figs into quarters and arrange them on a plate with the Parma ham. Garnish with the rocket.
40–50 minutes	Place the cherry tomatoes, still on the vine, in an ovenproof dish. Drizzle with the remaining oil and put them in the oven for about 10 minutes.
	Place the pineapple chunks in a serving bowl and chill in the fridge.
50–60 minutes	Take the potatoes out of the oven, toss and return to the oven.
	Preheat to the grill to medium.
	Melt the butter in a saucepan. Add the lemon juice, capers and mustard. Season with a little pepper. Place the mackerel fillets on a grill rack. Spoon about 1 tablespoon of the sauce on top each fillet. Sprinkle a pinch of sugar over the fillets then place them under the grill for about 6–8 minutes. Bring about 10ml water to the boil in a large saucepan. Remove the potatoes from the oven.
To serve	Put the plate of figs and ham on the table so that your guests can help themselves.
	Add a little salt to the saucepan of boiling water and then add the spinach. Cook, stirring constantly, for about 45 seconds, allowing just enough time for the spinach to wilt.
	Place the potatoes in a serving dish on the table, and do the same with the spinach. Put the remaining caper sauce in a serving dish. Serve each person a portion of mackerel with a couple of tomatoes still on the vine.
	Serve the pineapple chilled, with some yoghurt.
...and to drink	*Californian Chardonnay or Gaillac*

Family Reunion

True raclette is usually served as half a wheel of cheese, which is placed under an electric grill at the table, and the melted cheese is scraped off onto your plates. I have very fond childhood memories of this. I am not that sure if I was at all fond of the cheese but the ritual of eating the raclette was fun. As not everyone has a raclette grill I have adapted the recipe so that everyone can enjoy this delicious cheese. If you are on holiday in France you will find sliced raclette cheese in any supermarket. I usually pick up a couple of packets and freeze it until needed.

* € or €–€€ depending on cheese prices

€ or €–€€ *

Raclette with salad

Blackberry and almond tortaline

2kg waxy potatoes

1.2kg raclette cheese, sliced, skin on

2 tbsp olive oil

4 garlic cloves

salt and pepper

Salad

2 scallions (spring onions)

2 heads lettuce

cornichons, to serve

Dressing

3 tbsp olive oil

1 tbsp red wine vinegar

1 tsp Dijon mustard

1 tsp runny honey

salt and pepper

230ml double cream

2 tbsp icing sugar

2 tbsp white rum

100g chopped almonds

100g Amaretti biscuits

10–12 large blackberries, for decorating

Put a large saucepan of lightly salted water on to boil.

Slice the potatoes into rounds about 1cm thick, place in a steamer set over the saucepan of boiling water and steam for about 8 minutes.

Spread out the oil in the base of a large gratin dish. Remove the potatoes from the steamer and place about half of them in the dish in a single layer.

10–20 minutes

Preheat the oven to 200°C/400°F/Gas Mark 6.

20–30 minutes

Sprinkle half the garlic over the layer of potatoes, season with a little salt and pepper and put a layer of cheese on top. Now repeat with the remaining potatoes, garlic and cheese and season to taste. Cover with foil and place in the oven for about 25 minutes.

Using an electric whisk, whisk the cream and the icing sugar together until stiff. Gently stir in the rum, then fold in the almonds. Line a bun tin with decorative paper cases.

30–40 minutes

Place 2 Amaretti biscuits in the base of each paper case. Add a dollop of the cream mixture to the top of each and finish off with a blackberry. Place the tin in the freezer for about 1 hour.

40–50 minutes

Remove the foil from the raclette, increase the oven temperature to 220°C/425°F/Gas Mark 7 and bake for a further 10 minutes until the cheese starts to bubble and brown on top.

50–60 minutes

For the salad: Mix all the ingredients for the dressing together in a jar. Slice the scallions diagonally.

Place the lettuce and scallions in a large bowl.

Add the dressing to the salad, toss and serve with the raclette, accompanied by the cornichons.

To serve

Remove the tortaline from the freezer a few minutes before serving and place them on a decorative cake platter.

Gewürztraminer   **...and to drink**

Sunday Game

€–€€

This menu is ideal for an easy afternoon lunch or dinner. The almond and orange cake is a little oily and tacky in texture – a bit like a Tunisian orange cake.

Aperitif with a selection of olives

Tagliatelle with blue cheese and a crisp green salad with a raspberry vinaigrette dressing

---

Sweet almond and orange cake

olives mixed with red peppers,
capers, roasted garlic
and almond flakes

500g dried tagliatelle pasta
100g Cashel Blue cheese
300ml double cream
50ml milk
100g stoned dates
2 egg yolks
100g pine kernels
salt and pepper
handful snipped chives,
to garnish

Crisp green alad

mixed green salad leaves
½ red onion, finely chopped
handful fresh basil, to garnish

Dressing

1 small garlic clove, crushed
3 tbsp olive oil
1 tbsp raspberry vinegar
1 tsp Dijon mustard
1 tsp maple syrup
salt and freshly cracked
black pepper

250g butter, softened, plus
extra for greasing
250g caster sugar
4 eggs
grated rind and juice
of 1 orange
100g plain flour
100g ground almonds
icing sugar, for dusting

0–10 minutes

Preheat the oven to 180°C/350°F/Gas Mark 4.

Cream the butter and sugar together. Add the eggs, 1 at a time, and mix well to a smooth consistency. Add the orange rind and half the juice to the creamed butter and sugar.

10–20 minutes	Sift in the flour and stir in the almonds. Grease a 20-cm cake tin with a little butter and line with baking paper. Put the mixture into the cake tin. Put the cake in the oven for 30 minutes.
20–30 minutes	Tear the salad leaves and toss with the onion in a large bowl.
	For the dressing: Cut the garlic clove in half, remove and discard the inner stem and crush the rest of the clove. Mix all the dressing ingredients in a jar.
30–40 minutes	Break up the cheese. Place the pine kernels on a baking tray, put into the oven and toast for about 5 minutes.
40–50 minutes	Chop the dates into small pieces. Pour the cream into a heavy-based saucepan and place over a low heat. As soon as it starts to bubble around the edges stir in the cheese and milk. Season with salt and pepper.
50–60 minutes	Remove the cake from the oven and, while it is still warm, drizzle over the remaining orange juice. Set aside to cool.
	Bring a large saucepan of lightly salted water to the boil, add the pasta, bring back to the boil and cook for about 8–10 minutes. Drain the pasta and return it to the saucepan. Over a low heat, stir in the cheese sauce. Add the dates and season with salt and pepper. When the pasta is coated in the sauce remove from the heat and mix in the egg yolks and pine kernels.
To serve	Serve the olives with drinks.
	Serve each person a portion of pasta and finish the dish by sprinkling it with the chives.
	Dress and toss the salad and garnish with basil.
	Remove the cake from the tin, dust with some icing sugar and serve.
...and to drink	*Cabernet* *Muscat, to finish*

Making an Impression

Cutting the salmon fillets can be a little bit time-consuming and difficult. If you are not confident enough to try this your local fishmonger should be more than happy to help. If you want to spice up the dish rub a little wasabi on the inside of the salmon. The trifle is not really your typical trifle but I always hated the cold custard so I have left it out and created a creamy filling that goes really well with autumn berries.

€€

Aperitif with a mixture of nuts and small crackers

Asian salmon parcels with a soy and ginger sauce

Autumn fruits trifle

nuts

crackers

1 carrot

3 scallions (spring onions)

1 red pepper

½ white cabbage

1 red onion, finely sliced

1 handful beansprouts

1 tbsp lime juice

450g Thai rice

1 whole salmon cut into thin
    fillets about 12–14cm
    wide and 22–23cm long

olive oil, for brushing

2 tbsp chopped fresh coriander

2 tbsp chopped fresh mint

fresh coriander leaves
    and 2 limes, cut into
    wedges, to garnish

salt and pepper

Soy and ginger sauce

200ml white wine

200ml soy sauce

1 garlic clove, finely grated

2 tsp grated root ginger

½ red chilli

2 tbsp brown sugar

2 tbsp runny honey

6 tbsp blackberry jam

6 tbsp brandy

9 boudoir biscuits

350g fresh berries
    (blueberries, blackberries
    and raspberries)

250g mascarpone cheese

50g icing sugar

2 tbsp vanilla sugar

3 tbsp single cream

whipped cream, to decorate

0–10 minutes Put the jam into a small saucepan and place over a low heat. Add 4 tablespoons of the brandy to the jam.

Break a boudoir biscuit into the base of each of 6 glasses. Put a little of the warm jam over the biscuit base and then pile some of the fruit on top, until the glass is about two-thirds full.

Beat the mascarpone cheese, icing sugar and vanilla sugar together. Soften the mixture by adding some cream. Spread a little of the mixture evenly over the fruit in the glasses. Place the glasses on a tray and chill in the fridge.

10–20 minutes

Slice the carrot into thin matchsticks. Slice the scallions and finely slice the onion. Finely slice the pepper and shred the cabbage. Mix all the vegetables together and drizzle with a little lime juice. Add the coriander and mint and mix with the vegetables.

20–30 minutes

Hold firmly on to the tail of the salmon and, using a very sharp long-bladed fish knife, cut about 3 fillets from each side. Run the knife the whole length of the fish.

30–40 minutes

Preheat the oven to 200°C/400°F/Gas Mark 6.

40–50 minutes

Bring a large saucepan of lightly salted water to the boil. Add the rice and cook for about 15–18 minutes until tender.

Lay each salmon fillet flat, season with salt and pepper and place a portion of the vegetable mixture down the centre of each fillet. Roll up the fillets and place on a baking tray. Brush with a little oil, place them in the oven and cook for about 12–15 minutes.

For the sauce: Combine the wine and soy sauce in a saucepan. Add the garlic and ginger. Deseed and finely slice the chilli. Add this to the sauce along with the sugar and honey. Bring the sauce to bubbling, reduce the heat and simmer for about 5 minutes. Drain the rice in a sieve and rinse through with boiling water. Strain the sauce.

50–60 minutes

Serve the nuts and crackers with some drinks.

To serve

Serve each person a portion of salmon and rice with a little sauce, garnished with a lime wedge.

Serve straight from the fridge, decorated with a small blob of whipped cream and some berries.

Australian Riesling

...and to drink

Lunch for the Girls

€–€€

It was Annie, a friend I did a cooking course with in France, who introduced me to this excellent pie. Instead of filo she used a North African type of pastry called *bric*. Although it takes a little bit of time to assemble the pie the end result is excellent. You don't have to use the vegetables I've specified – feel free to add what you like. The only must-do is that you brush each side of the filo pastry with oil – otherwise it won't crisp up. The sticky toffee muffins were made on the *Yumee* show and have always been a firm favourite with my girlfriends.

Aperitif with cashew nuts

Annie's aubergine, courgette and goat's cheese filo loaf and a green salad with a sweet balsamic dressing

---

Sticky toffee muffins with toffee sauce and vanilla ice cream

cashew nuts

2 onions
2 courgettes
1 aubergine
1 red pepper
2 tomatoes
1 garlic clove, crushed
150g goat's cheese
8 tbsp olive oil, plus
    extra for brushing
50g Parmesan cheese, grated
1 tsp mixed herbs
6 eggs
100ml milk

260g readymade filo pastry
    sheets (6 sheets)
salt and pepper

Salad
2 heads lettuce

Dressing
6 tbsp olive oil
1 tbsp balsamic vinegar
1 tsp tarragon vinegar
1–2 tsp runny honey
1 tsp Dijon mustard
salt and pepper

100g butter, softened
150g soft light brown sugar
2 eggs
175g plain white flour
1 tsp baking powder
175g stoned chopped dates
150ml warm water
1 tsp vanilla extract

Toffee sauce
100g butter
125g soft light brown sugar
100ml single cream
50g walnuts

0–10 minutes	Soak the dates in the warm water with the vanilla extract.
	Slice the onion. Cut the courgettes and the aubergine into small cubes. Deseed the pepper and thinly slice. Slice the tomatoes. Heat about 2 tablespoons of the oil in a wok or large frying pan. Quick-fry the onions, then add the courgettes, aubergine, red pepper, tomatoes and garlic. Stir-fry for about 8 minutes. Add the mixed herbs and season with a pinch of salt and pepper.
10–20 minutes	Preheat the oven to 190°C/375°F/Gas Mark 5.
	Lightly beat 5 whole eggs and 1 egg yolk together. Add the milk and gently mix with a fork. Put the remaining oil into a small dish. Remove the vegetables from the heat

and set aside to cool. Cut the pastry sheets in half. Brush each side with oil and lay 4 sheets, one on top of the other, in the base of a baking dish. Place half the vegetables on top of the pastry. Scatter half the goat's cheese over the vegetables.

Pour half the egg mixture over the vegetables and add 4 more layers of filo pastry, brushing each sheet on both sides with oil. Put the remaining vegetables and goat's cheese on top of the pastry. Pour the remaining egg mixture over the vegetables, topped off with some grated Parmesan cheese. Fold the sheets of pastry over the vegetables and top off the dish with 4 more layers of filo pastry, not forgetting to brush each side of each sheet with oil. Put the loaf on the middle shelf of the oven and bake for about 35 minutes.

20–30 minutes

Cream the butter and sugar together. Add the eggs one at a time to the creamed butter and sugar and beat them in using a wooden spoon. Add the baking powder to the flour and sift into the creamed butter and sugar mixture. Add the dates and mix well.

30–40 minutes

Line a 6-hole muffin tin with paper cases. Scoop the mixture into the cases and put in the oven to bake for about 20–25 minutes.

40–50 minutes

Combine the butter, sugar, cream and walnuts in a small saucepan. Warm slightly until all the sugar has melted and you are left with a sticky sauce. Set aside for later.

50–60 minutes

Mix all the dressing ingredients together in a large bowl. Tear the lettuce leaves and toss in the dressing.

Serve the cashew nuts with some drinks.

To serve

Serve the pie warm from the oven with the salad on the side.

Remove the muffins from the oven and set aside to cool slightly. Peel away the paper cases. Heat the sauce. Serve each person a muffin drizzled with sauce, with a scoop of vanilla ice cream on the side.

Barbera or Cabernet-Shiraz   **...and to drink**

Lunch for Mother-in-Law

€–€€

This is an ideal lunch menu. It's a favourite of my mother's and everyone always raves about the sauce.

Aperitif with a selection of olives

Lemon paprika chicken with long-grain and wild rice

Mixed leaf salad

Apple and ricotta pastry parcels

selection of olives

1 tbsp runny honey
juice of ½ lemon
½ tbsp Worcestershire sauce
1 tbsp Dijon mustard
1½ tbsp paprika
6 small chicken fillets
500g easy-cook mixed long-
  grain and wild rice
sunflower oil, for frying
230ml single cream
butter, for dressing the rice
salt and pepper
fresh parsley, to garnish

1 bag mixed salad leaves
handful baby leaf spinach
handful dandelion leaves
snipped chives

Dressing
4 tbsp olive oil
2 tbsp rapeseed oil
2 tbsp red wine vinegar
1 large tsp Dijon mustard
1 tsp runny honey
salt and pepper

3 eating apples
1 tsp lemon juice
2 tbsp Calvados
2 tbsp caster sugar
½ tsp ground cinnamon
1 tbsp raisins
425g ready-rolled puff
  pastry (2 sheets)
6 tsp ricotta cheese
1 egg, beaten
pouring cream or crème
  fraîche, to serve

0–10 minutes

Peel and core the apples and cut into small neat chunks. Drizzle with the lemon juice and Calvados and sprinkle with the caster sugar and cinnamon. Mix well and add the raisins. Take the pastry out of the fridge.

10–20 minutes	Mix together the honey, lemon juice, Worcestershire sauce, mustard and paprika and spread out on the base of a flat dish. Lay the chicken breasts on a clean chopping board. Cover with clingfilm and gently bash with a rolling pin to flatten.
20–30 minutes	Season the chicken breasts on both sides with a little salt and pepper and then spread each one with some of the lemon-paprika mixture. Leave to marinate for at least 30 minutes. Mix all the dressing ingredients together in a jar.

Bring a large saucepan of lightly salted water to the boil.

Open out the pastry and cut each sheet in quarters.

Add a pinch of salt to the water. Rinse the rice under cold running water and add to the saucepan of boiling water. Return to the boil and simmer for 16 minutes, until the rice is just barely cooked – the grains should still be slightly crunchy.

Put a heaped teaspoon of ricotta cheese in the centre of each pastry square and then add about a tablespoon of the apple and raisin mixture. Brush the borders with some of the apple and raisin juices and scrunch the sides of the squares together, making 8 little parcels. Line a baking tray with baking paper and set the parcels on the tray. Lightly brush each parcel with the beaten egg. Place the tray of parcels in the fridge.

Heat a little oil in a large non-stick frying pan.

Drain the rice in a sieve and rinse through with a kettle of boiling water. Put the rice in a serving dish and add about 3 small knobs of butter. Mix well, cover with foil and place in a low oven.

Add the chicken breasts to the frying pan and gently fry for about 2 minutes on each side. Mix the cream with the leftover marinade. Pour the paprika cream into the pan around the chicken. Allow to bubble, reduce the heat and cook for about 6–8 minutes.

Serve a selection of olives with drinks.

Garnish the chicken with parsley and serve with the rice and lemon wedges.

Dress and toss the salad and serve with the chicken.

Preheat the oven to 200°C/400°F/Gas Mark 6. Remove the chilled pastry parcels from the fridge and place in the oven for about 20 minutes. Serve warm, straight from the oven, with some pouring cream.

30–40 minutes

40–50 minutes

50–60 minutes

To Serve

Semillon Riesling Chardonnay   **...and to drink**

Bloke's Night In

€ For Halloween night mum would always have a pot of chilli on the stove. It's great to have just in case you have extra visitors. I recommend beer with this meal or a delicious margarita. This is a great dinner to make if you plan to watch a movie or match or even just have a party.

Chicken wings

Texas chilli served with tortillas

20 chicken wings	1–2 large onions, chopped	50g Cheddar cheese, sliced
4 tbsp honey	2 green peppers, deseeded	
1 tbsp mustard	and sliced	**Salsa**
3 tbsp soy sauce	2 green or red chillies,	2 vine-ripened tomatoes
1½ tsp cayenne pepper	chopped, but not deseeded	1 small red onion
2 tbsp tomato ketchup	800g canned chopped	3 tbsp chopped fresh coriander
3 tbsp sunflower oil	tomatoes	juice of ½ lime
4 tbsp chopped fresh	1–2 tsp cumin	salt and pepper
coriander, to garnish	400g canned red kidney	
	beans, drained	**To garnish**
650g round steak mince	1 tsp brown sugar	100g crème fraîche
2 tbsp olive oil	salt and pepper	100g natural yoghurt
2 garlic cloves, crushed	8 flour tortillas (8 in a packet)	3 tbsp chopped fresh coriander

0–10 minutes   Remove the chicken wing tips and discard. Mix the honey, mustard, soy sauce, cayenne pepper, ketchup and oil together in a large flat dish. Reserve a third of the marinade. Toss the wings in about two thirds of the marinade. Cover with clingfilm and place in the fridge to marinate.

10–20 minutes   Heat the oil in a large casserole dish or saucepan. Add the mince and cook until browned.

Preheat the oven to 200°C/400°F/Gas Mark 6.

20–30 minutes   Add the onion and garlic and cook for about a minute. Add the peppers, chillies and canned tomatoes and season with salt. Cover, bring to the boil and simmer for about 30 minutes.

30–40 minutes   Place the chicken wings in a single layer on a baking tray, place in the oven and cook for about 25 minutes.

For the salsa: Chop the tomatoes, finely chop the onion and mix together. Add the coriander and the lime juice and mix well.

40–50 minutes   Lay a flour tortilla on a plate. Spoon about 1 tablespoon of the salsa onto the edge of the tortilla, then lay a slice of cheese on top and roll up the tortilla. Repeat this for all the tortillas, place them on a baking tray and bake in the oven for about 6–8 minutes.

50–60 minutes   Take the chicken wings out of the oven and drizzle them with the remaining sauce.

Toss well in the remaining sauce and put them back in the oven for another 8–10 minutes or until cooked.

Add the cumin, kidney beans and sugar. Simmer for a further 10 minutes. Taste and season.

To serve   Take the chicken wings out of the oven and scatter with fresh coriander. Serve on a large platter.

Mix the crème fraîche, yoghurt and coriander together. Serve each person a portion of chilli, topped with a dollop of the crème fraîche mixture, some grated cheese and a sprinkling of fresh coriander with a tortilla on the side.

...and to drink   *Beer or margaritas*

Casual Midweek Dinner

This is a straightforward meal, nothing frilly. The roasted vegetables are so versatile they can be served with any type of meat or fish. The added bonus is less cleaning of pots if you roast all the vegetables in one tray. The salad is a twist on the traditional English Stilton and walnut salad. Adding blueberries lifts the colour of the salad and their tangy juicy bite is an excellent accompaniment to the Cashel Blue cheese.

€–€€

Lamb chops with roast vegetables, new potatoes and Dijon mustard

Cashel Blue, blueberry and walnut salad

Meringue nests with ricotta vanilla cream and fresh fruit with a blueberry coulis

2 red onions

1 red pepper

1 green pepper

1 yellow pepper

12 button mushrooms

6 tomatoes

3 tbsp olive oil

1 tsp dried basil

1 tsp dried oregano

1kg new potatoes

2 tbsp sunflower oil

6 loin lamb chops, about
   1kg (or 2 per person
   if they are small)

butter, for dressing
   the potatoes

2 tbsp snipped chives

salt and pepper

100g Cashel Blue cheese

2 heads lettuce (different types)

150g blueberries

150g walnuts

rustic bread, to serve

Dressing

6 tbsp olive oil

2 tbsp balsamic vinegar

1 tsp Dijon mustard

1 tsp runny honey

salt and pepper

150g strawberries

150g raspberries

150g blueberries

1 tbsp lemon juice

2 tsp caster sugar

2 tbsp icing sugar

250g ricotta cheese

150ml single cream

1½ tsp vanilla extract

6 meringue nests

275g bottled blueberry coulis

0–10 minutes	Remove the cheese from its wrapping and arrange on a plate. Leave to stand at room temperature but keep covered.
	Cut the onions into quarters. Deseed the peppers and cut into large chunks. Wipe the mushrooms clean with some damp kitchen paper. Cut the tomatoes into quarters.
10–20 minutes	Put all the vegetables into a large ovenproof dish.
	Hull and quarter the strawberries. Cut the raspberries in half. Mix all the fruit together in a large bowl and add the lemon juice and sugar. Cover the bowl and place in the fridge.
	Preheat the oven to 190°C/375°F/Gas Mark 5.
20–30 minutes	Bring a large saucepan of lightly salted water to the boil. Drizzle the vegetables with olive oil. Sprinkle the basil and oregano over the vegetables. Add some salt and pepper. Toss all the vegetables with the oil and seasoning using your fingers. Put the vegetables in the oven for about 30 minutes.
30–40 minutes	Put the potatoes in a steamer set over the saucepan of boiling water.
	Tear the lettuce and place in a bowl with about 150g blueberries. Crumble in the cheese and the walnuts. In a separate dish, mix all the dressing ingredients together. Put the salad into the fridge.
40–50 minutes	Cream the icing sugar and ricotta cheese together. Use the cream to thin the mixture slightly. When you have a rich creamy texture add the vanilla extract and mix well. Put in the fridge until ready to serve.
	Heat a little oil in 2 frying pans and add the chops.
50–60 minutes	Cook the chops, frying for about 4 minutes on each side.
	Put the mustard into a serving dish.

To serve Remove the potatoes from the oven and place them in a warmed serving dish. Add the butter and chives and lightly toss. Place the vegetables on the table. Serve each person a chop on a warmed plate.

Add the dressing to the salad and toss. Slice the bread.

Arrange the meringues on a serving platter or cake stand. Remove the ricotta cream from the fridge and put about a tablespoon in the centre of each meringue. Top with some fruit and then drizzle with the blueberry coulis.

...and to drink *Mature Bordeaux*

Candlelight Dinner

This is a light enough meal, ideal for a romantic night with a bit of spice. Although the main course may seem a little hot, the sweetness of the teriyaki sauce calms all the flavours, and the nerves. The apricot compôte, bursting with juice, is ideal to finish, and the sweetness of the vanilla will leave everyone feeling warm and loved.

€–€€

Aperitif with prawn crackers and a sweet chilli dipping sauce

---

Sweet chilli salmon cakes, coriander rice with a teriyaki chilli sauce and baby spinach

---

Vanilla and apricot compôte with vanilla ice cream

prawn crackers

bottled sweet chilli
   dipping sauce

5 salmon fillets, or about
   650g skinless, boneless
   fresh salmon

2 tbsp sweet chilli sauce

handful chopped fresh
   coriander

juice of ½ lemon

450g basmati rice

olive oil, for brushing

4 knobs butter

500g baby leaf spinach

salt and pepper

Teriyaki chilli sauce

200ml soy sauce

200ml white wine

1 tsp grated root ginger

1 tsp grated garlic

1 red chilli, deseeded
   and finely chopped

2 tbsp brown sugar

2 tbsp runny honey

250ml water

1kg apricots

250g caster sugar

1 vanilla pod

**1 tub good quality vanilla
   ice cream, to serve**

Put the water in a heavy-based saucepan and bring to the boil. Halve and stone the apricots. Add the sugar to the boiling water, stir well and return to the boil.

0–10 minutes

Add the apricots and the vanilla pod. Cover the saucepan, reduce the heat and simmer gently for about 15 minutes.

10–20 minutes

For the sauce: Put the soy sauce and wine into a separate small saucepan. Add the ginger, garlic, chilli, sugar and honey. Bring to the boil. When it bubbles reduce the heat and leave to simmer for about 3 minutes. Remove from the heat and allow all the flavours to combine.

20–30 minutes

Cut the salmon into large chunks. Remove any bones. Mince the salmon in a food processor, adding the sweet chilli sauce, half the coriander and the lemon juice and season with a little salt and pepper.

30–40 minutes

Remove the apricots from the heat and set aside to cool.

Form the minced salmon into 6 hamburger-sized cakes. Cover them with clingfilm and put in the fridge. Bring a large saucepan of lightly salted water to the boil.

40–50 minutes

Preheat the oven to 190°C/375°F/Gas Mark 5.

Rinse the rice under cold running water. Add to the saucepan of boiling water, stir and cover. Bring back to the boil, reduce the heat and simmer for about 7 minutes, just until the rice still has some crunch. Bring a full kettle of water to the boil. Brush a baking tray with some olive oil and place the salmon cakes on the tray.

Put the salmon cakes in the oven and cook for about 12–15 minutes.

50–60 minutes

Bring 200ml water to the boil in a saucepan. Add 2 knobs of butter.

Drain the rice and pour some boiling water through it. Put the rice into a large bowl. Add 2–3 knobs of butter and the remaining coriander and fluff with a fork. Cover the bowl with foil and place in the bottom of the oven. When the salmon cakes are cooked, reduce the oven temperature to low and allow the rice to cook for about 4–5 minutes.

To serve

Serve the prawn crackers with a little sweet chilli sauce for dipping.

Add a little salt to the saucepan of boiling water and then add the spinach. Cook, stirring constantly, for about 45 seconds until the spinach wilts.

Strain the sauce through a sieve, place in a saucepan over a low heat and heat slightly. Add the slices of red chilli to the sauce at the last minute. Put a salmon cake, some rice and some spinach on each plate and drizzle a little sauce over the rice. Garnish with some coriander.

Remove the vanilla pod from the apricots (wash and dry the pod and store for future use) and serve them slightly warm with some good quality vanilla ice cream.

...and to drink   *Semillon Sauvignon Blanc*

Alternative Sunday Dinner

The meatloaf is my mother's recipe. It's great family lunch that's cheap, and the kids will love it, especially with the sweet barbecue sauce.

€

Meatloaf with roast potatoes, broccoli and a comforting white sauce

Apple pie

12 potatoes (Irish Roosters)

2 tbsp olive oil

2 onions, finely chopped

425g round steak mince

225g sausage meat

2 handfuls porridge oats

1 tbsp tomato purée

3 carrots, grated

2 handfuls of raisins

1 large egg

350g broccoli florets

salt and pepper

cherry tomatoes, to garnish

Barbecue sauce

4 tbsp soy sauce

5 tbsp tomato ketchup

2 tbsp runny honey

1 tsp Worcestershire sauce

salt and pepper

White sauce

30g butter

30g flour

400ml milk

20g white Cheddar cheese

salt and pepper

6 large Bramley apples

4–6 tbsp caster sugar

1 tsp cinnamon

450g ready-to-roll
**   shortcrust pastry**

butter, for greasing

1 egg

1 tbsp milk

pouring cream or vanilla
**   ice cream, to serve**

Preheat the oven to 190°C/375°F/Gas Mark 5.

0–10 minutes

Using a fork pierce a couple of holes in the potatoes. Heat the oil in a saucepan and soften the onion until it's transparent.

Put the potatoes on a baking tray and place in the oven.

10–20 minutes

Remove the onion from the heat and allow to cool. Put the mince, sausage meat, oats, tomato purée, grated carrot, raisins, onions and egg into a large mixing bowl and mix with your hands. Season with a little salt and pepper. Divide the mixture in half and shape each half into a large loaf. Put the loaves on a baking tray.

20–30 minutes

For the barbecue sauce: Put the soy sauce and ketchup into a saucepan over a low heat. Cook, stirring constantly, until they combine. Sweeten the sauce with some honey. Add the Worcestershire sauce and season with a little salt and pepper. Adjust the seasoning to taste. Spoon half the sauce over each meat loaf. Pour about 100ml water into the bottom of the tray. Loosely cover the meat loaves with foil and then put them in the oven for about 35–40 minutes.

30–40 minutes

Peel and core the apples and put them into a large saucepan with 150ml water, 4 tablespoons of the caster sugar and the cinnamon. Cover and cook for about 5 minutes, or until the apples are soft but still maintain their shape.

40–50 minutes

Divide the pastry in half and, using a floured rolling pin, roll it out. Grease the baking dish with a little butter and line with the pastry. Add the apples. Sprinkle a little sugar over them to taste. Roll out the other half of the pastry and use this to cover the apples. Make four small slits in the top of the pastry. Mix the egg with the milk and brush the pastry with the mixture. Put the pie in the oven and cook for about 35–40 minutes.

50–60 minutes

Remove the potatoes from the oven and cover with a clean dry tea towel to keep them.

Remove the foil from the meatloaves and allow the tops to brown.

Bring a kettle of water to the boil and add boiling water to a steamer. Put the broccoli into the top half of the steamer and put the steamer on the hob over a medium heat.

For the white sauce: Melt the butter in a saucepan. Remove from the heat and stir in the flour. Return the saucepan to the heat and cook gently for a minute. Add the milk and whisk. Bring the sauce to a simmer, whisking to remove any lumps. Remove the sauce from the heat and add the grated cheese, a little at a time, whisking constantly. Season with salt and pepper

Remove the meatloaves and potatoes from the oven and move the pie to the top half of the oven. Remove the broccoli from the steamer and put in a serving dish.

To serve   Put the potatoes in a serving dish. Place the broccoli and the potatoes on the table. Give each person 2 slices of meatloaf with some white sauce and garnish with tomatoes.

When the pastry is golden brown and crisp on top the pie is cooked. Remove from the oven and leave to stand for a couple of minutes before serving so that it's warm but not piping hot. Serve with pouring cream.

...and to drink   *Tempranillo*

Something a Bit Cheffy

Stuffing the chicken breast can be a little bit tricky at first but once you get the hang of it nothing will hold you back. Substitute various cheeses and other vegetables for a totally new dish. If you like lemon curd then you will love this dessert.

€–€€

Chicken breast stuffed with Brie and leeks, wrapped in smoked pancetta

Green salad with a French dressing

Lemon syllabub

500g baby potatoes	2 heads lettuce (different types)	3 lemons
3 leeks	½ fennel bulb	3 tbsp sweet white wine
150g Brie		150–200g icing sugar
6 skinless chicken breasts, about 125g each	**Dressing**	450ml double cream
	6 tbsp olive oil	fresh mint leaves, to decorate
115g smoked pancetta or smoked streaky bacon rashers	2 tbsp white wine vinegar	shortbread biscuits, to serve
	1 tbsp Dijon mustard	
	1 tbsp maple syrup	
4 tomatoes	salt and pepper	
4 tbsp olive oil, for frying		
salt and pepper		

Fill the bottom part of a steamer with water and bring to the boil. Slice the potatoes into small rounds.

0–10 minutes

Bring a large saucepan of lightly salted water to the boil.

Cut the leeks in half lengthways.

10–20 minutes   Put the potatoes into the top part of the steamer, place it over the boiling water and steam for about 8 minutes.

Blanch the leeks in the boiling water for about a minute, remove from the water and chop. Put a third of the chopped leek in a bowl, mix with the Brie and season with a little salt and pepper.

Remove the potatoes from the steamer.

20–30 minutes   Using a very sharp knife carefully butterfly the chicken breasts by cutting through them horizontally (the chicken should still be in one piece). Spread a small amount of the Brie and leek mixture lengthways along the centre of each chicken breast. Fold over the chicken breasts and then wrap 2 slices of smoked pancetta around each one. They will look a little bit like croissants.

30–40 minutes   Slice the tomatoes. Thinly slice half the fennel bulb.

40–50 minutes   Grate the zest of 1 lemon and squeeze the juice of 3 lemons. Mix the lemon zest, lemon juice, wine and 150g icing sugar together. Place the cream in a food mixer and start to whisk. Spoon in the lemon, wine and sugar mixture, a little at a time, while the mixer is still going. Keep whisking until it holds its shape. Taste and add more icing sugar if required. Spoon into individual glasses and put the glasses in the fridge.

Preheat the oven to 200°C/400°F/Gas Mark 6.

50–60 minutes   Dry-fry the chicken in a large frying pan for about 2–3 minutes until starting to brown. Transfer to the oven for 6–8 minutes until cooked through.

Heat 2 tablespoons of the oil in a large frying pan. Fry the potatoes, then add the sliced tomatoes and the remaining leeks. Drizzle with the balsamic vinegar and a tablespoon of the oil.

To serve   Serve each person a portion of the potatoes, tomatoes and leeks with a chicken breast on top.

Mix all the dressing ingredients together in a jar. Put the lettuce into a large bowl, dress and toss.

Decorate the top of each syllabub with a mint leaf. Serve each person a syllabub with a shortbread biscuit and a glass of Muscat on the side.

...and to drink   *White Burgundy*
                          Muscat, to finish

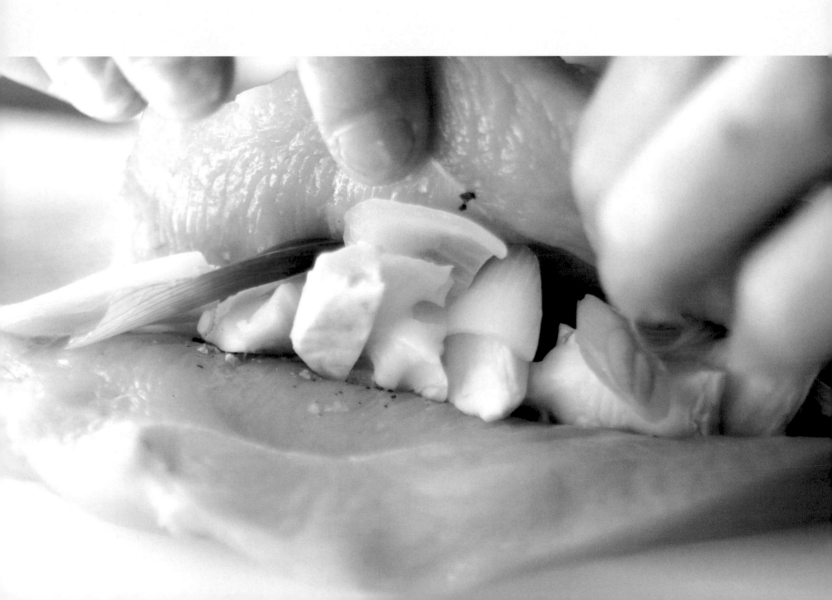

Oozing Sophistication

Quitterie was a French student who came to work on the farm in summer 2006. Chocolate fondants are her speciality. She showed me this simple way to make an exquisite dessert with no extra folding or mixing – the fondants don't even need a bain marie. Her method is so easy we spent the entire summer making them with different centres. You could put a square of white chocolate or a cherry soaked in brandy in the centre.

€€–€€€

Poulet au vin

Salad with cheese

Quitterie's chocolate fondants and vanilla ice cream

1kg new potatoes

8 button mushrooms

1 kg chicken thighs,
    about 8–10 thighs

2 tbsp olive oil

2 garlic cloves, roughly
    chopped

8 small shallots,
    roughly chopped

6 slices smoked
    pancetta, diced

2 sprigs fresh thyme

150ml red wine

150ml chicken stock

1 bay leaf

1 tsp herbes de Provence

handful fresh parsley,
    finely chopped

salt and pepper

2 heads lettuce (different types)

2 scallions (spring
    onions), finely sliced

Brie

Camembert

Cashel Blue

1 French stick

Dressing

4 tbsp olive oil

1½ tbsp cider vinegar

1 tsp Dijon mustard

1 tsp runny honey

salt and pepper

150g plain chocolate,
    with at least 60–70 per
    cent cocoa solids

100g butter, plus extra
    for greasing

3 eggs

1 tsp vanilla extract

125g sugar

1 tbsp flour

good quality vanilla ice
    cream, to serve

0–10 minutes	Take the cheeses out of their wrappings and arrange on a plate. Leave to stand at room temperature before serving.

Cut the potatoes into quarters. Wipe the mushrooms clean and slice.

Remove any excess skin from the chicken thighs. |
| **10–20 minutes** | Heat the oil in a large saucepan until hot, then add the chicken thighs, skin side down, and brown. Turn and brown slightly on the other side. Pour the fat out of the saucepan. Place the pancetta, shallots and garlic in the same saucepan. Toss and cook until the pancetta is slightly browned. Add the mushrooms and thyme and cook for about 1 minute. Pour in the wine and chicken stock. Add the bay leaf and the herbes de Provence. Return the chicken to the saucepan, add the potatoes and season with salt and pepper. Cover and simmer for about 40–50 minutes. |
| **20–30 minutes** | Melt 125g chocolate with the butter in the microwave for 30 seconds on Medium. Stir and cook for a further 30–45 seconds. Add the eggs, one at a time, using a hand balloon whisk to beat them in. Add the vanilla extract, sugar and flour and beat well with the whisk. |

30–40 minutes	Fold a large piece of baking paper in half a couple of times so that you end up with 6 folds. Place an individual pudding mould on the baking paper and draw around the rim. Cut out the circular shape. You should end up with 6 paper circles. Grease 6 metal fondant moulds with a little butter and place a paper circle in the base of each. Dust each mould with a little flour.
40–50 minutes	Fill each mould about two-thirds full, then place a square of chocolate in the centre. Divide the remaining mixture between the moulds, place the moulds on a tray, cover with clingfilm and put into the fridge.
	Tear the lettuce.
50–60 minutes	Mix all the dressing ingredients together in a jar.
To serve	Turn off the heat under the chicken and leave to stand for about 8 minutes before serving. Taste and add the chopped parsley. Serve at the table in large individual bowls.
	Toss the salad in the dressing and serve it with the cheese and the bread.
	Preheat the oven to 200°C/400°F/Gas Mark 6. Transfer the chocolate fondants directly from the fridge to the oven and cook for about 10–12 minutes. As soon as you remove them from the oven, tip them onto small plates and serve immediately with some vanilla ice cream.
...and to drink	*Beaujolais Cru*

Index